WITHDRAWN
HARVARD LIBRARY
WITHDRAWN

BOSTON COLLEGE STUDIES IN PHILOSOPHY

EDITORIAL BOARD

FREDERICK J. ADELMANN
(*Editor*)

Donald A. Gallagher
Norman J. Wells
Thomas J. Blakeley
John P. Rock
Richard T. Murphy
Oliva Blanchette

Dedicated
to
JOHN WILD
1902–1972

a devoted teacher, a scholarly philosopher,
a Christian gentle-person

BOSTON COLLEGE STUDIES
IN PHILOSOPHY

VOLUME III

AUTHORITY

FREDERICK J. ADELMANN, S.J.
Editor

BOSTON COLLEGE
CHESTNUT HILL
1974

MARTINUS NIJHOFF
THE HAGUE
1974

© 1974 by Martinus Nijhoff, The Hague, Netherlands
All rights reserved, including the right to translate or to
reproduce this book or parts thereof in any form
ISBN 90 247 1594 6

PRINTED IN THE NETHERLANDS

ACKNOWLEDGMENTS

A special debt of gratitude is due to Darton, Longman & Todd, Ltd. of London, and to the Seabury Press of New York for permission to use the English translation of Karl Rahner's article by Graham Harrison which appears in *Theological Investigations*, Vol. IX, pp. 83–100, Herder and Herder, New York, 1972 and Darton, Longman & Todd, Ltd., London, 1972. Also the editor wishes to thank Professor Rahner and the Benziger Publishing House of Zurich for their kindness in this matter too.

Grateful acknowledgment is made to the following publishers who kindly granted permission to use quotations from the following works: to the MacMillan Company for permission to quote from Kenneth Megill's *The New Democratic Theory*; to Harper and Row, Publishers, Inc. for permission to quote from Robert Paul Wolff's *In Defence of Anarchism;* and to W. W. Norton and Company, Inc. for permission to quote from the *Marx-Engel's Reader*, edited by Professor Robert Tucker.

The editor would especially like to thank the distinguished contributors of these articles; also Mrs. Helen Fitzgerald who typed the manuscript; Professors Thomas J. Blakeley, Walter J. Feeney, S.J. and Stanley J. Bezuszka, S.J. for valuable aid and suggestions. Also the Reverends Frederick G. McLeod, S.J. and James F. Halpin, S.J. for reading my article and giving me academic encouragement. Finally and perhaps most of all to Miss Kathleen Wright, my graduate assistant who proofread the entire volume and attended to those myriad details that have finally brought the mission to a count-down.

The Editor
July 1, 1973

Boston College
Chestnut Hill, Mass. U.S.A.

CONTENTS

Contributors XI

FREDERICK J. ADELMANN, *Foreword* 1

JOHN WILD, *Authority* 7

BERNARD LONERGAN, *Dialectic of Authority* 24

RICHARD T. DE GEORGE, *Authority and Morality* 31

WILLIAM H. DAVIS, *Stooping to Conquer: Reflections on Authority* 50

JOSEPH M. BOCHENSKI, *An Analysis of Authority* 56

KARL RAHNER, *Theology and the Church's Teaching Authority after the Council* 86

FREDERICK J. ADELMANN, *Authority* 105

CONTRIBUTORS

Professor John Wild was born in Chicago, Ill. in 1902. He obtained his Ph.B. in philosophy from the University of Chicago in 1923, his M.A. from Harvard in 1925, and his Ph.D. from the University of Chicago in 1926. He began instructing philosophy at Harvard in 1927, where he remained until 1961, having obtained the rank of professor in 1946. From 1961 until 1963 Professor Wild taught at Northwestern University. From 1963 until his death in October 1972 Professor Wild taught at Yale University. Interested in the history of Greek philosophy, phenomenology and existential philosophy, his publications include: *Plato's Modern Enemies and the Theory of Natural Law; Challenge of Existentialism;* and *Existence and the World of Freedom.*

Professor Bernard Lonergan, S.J., was born in Buckingham, Quebec in 1904. He obtained his B.A. from the University of London and his S.T.D. from Gregorian University. He has been professor of theology at L'Immaculée Conception (Montreal), Regis College (Toronto) and Gregorian University. He is presently a Resident Professor at Regis College (Willowdale) as well as Aquinas Lecturer at Marquette University. During 1971–1972 he held the Stillman chair of theology at Havard University. His publications include: *Insight: a Study of Human Understanding; De Deo Trino; Collection: Papers by B. Lonergan; Verbum: Word and Idea in Aquinas; St. Thomas' Thought on Gratia Operans;* and *Method in Theology.*

Professor Richard De George was born in New York, New York in 1933. After obtaining his B.A. from Fordham he went on to Yale for a M.A. and Ph.D. in philosophy in 1959. He has taught at the University of Kansas since 1959 and presently holds the position of Professor. A member of the American Philosophical Association, the Metaphysical Society of America, the American Association for the Advancement of Slavic Studies and the American Catholic Philosophical Association, Professor De George has been active in the fields of Soviet philosophy, ethics and metaphysics. He has served as editor of "Classical and Contemporary Metaphysics," and *Ethics and Society* (Anchor Books, 1966). He is author of *Patterns of Soviet Thought; Soviet Ethics and Morality; The New Marxism;* "Dialectical Thought" (in *Reflections on Man*, Harcourt 1966); and co-author of *Science and Ideology in Soviet Society*.

Professor William H. Davis was born in Lincoln County, Tennessee in 1939. After obtaining his B.A. from Abilene Christian College, he continued his studies at Rice University, being awarded a M.A. and Ph.D. in philosophy in 1965. After two years as an Instructor at the University of Houston, Professor Davis holds at present the position of Assistant Professor at Auburn University. A member of the Southwest Philosophical Society, he has worked in the field of epistemology and on the philosophy of Charles S. Pierce. He is author of *Science and Christian Faith* and *The Free Will*.

Professor Joseph M. Bochenski, O.P., was born in Czuszow (Poland) in 1902. He studied law and political economy at the Universities of Lwow and Poznan, and later philosophy and pedagogics at the university of Fribourg in Switzerland, where he obtained his Ph.D. in philosophy. He was granted a D.D. from the Angelicum in Rome. Professor Bochenski has taught at the Angelicum, the University of Cracow, the University of Fribourg, the University of Cologne, the University of Notre Dame (Indiana), the University of California (L.A.) and the University of Kansas. His publications include: *de cognitione existentiae Dei; La Logique de Theophraste; Europaeische Philosophie der Gegenwart; Précis de Logique Mathematique; Der Sowetrussische Dialektische Materialismus; Ancient Formal Logic; Handbuch des Weltkommunismus; Logisch-philosophische Studien; Wege zur philosophischen Denken; The Logic of Religion;* and *Studies in Soviet Thought* (editor).

Professor Karl Rahner, S.J., was born in Freiburg i. Br. in 1904 and entered the Order of the Jesuits in 1922. From 1934 until 1936 he studied philosophy with Martin Heidegger at Freiburg i. Br. His Doctor of Theology was obtained from the University of Innsbruck in 1936. He has taught at the University of Innsbruck, the University of Vienna, the Jesuit University in Pullach, the University of Munich and finally at the University of Muenster/Westfalen where he has been Professor emeritus since 1971. Concentrating on the philosophy of religion, systematic theology and practical theology, his publications include: *Geist in Welt; Hoerer des Wortes; Schriften zur Theologie;* and *Sendung und Gnade.*

Professor Frederick J. Adelmann, S.J., was born in Norwood, Mass. in 1915. After obtaining his A.B. and M.A. at Boston College, and his S.T.L. at Weston College, he studied at St. Louis University where he was granted a Ph.D. in philosophy in 1955. He has been teaching at Boston College since 1942 and presently holds the position of Professor of philosophy. A member of the American Philosophical Association and the Jesuit Philosophical Association, Professor Adelmann has served as the editor of the "Boston College Studies in Phliosophy." He is author of *From Dialogue to Epilogue* and co-author of *Guide to Marxist Philosophy.*

FOREWORD

It seems evident to anyone giving thought to the matter, that at the root of contemporary social ruptures lies an attack on the theory and practice of authority. Marcuse's philosophy could be equated with anti-authoritarianism. His anti-establishment theses cut deeply into the roots of every contemporary institutional structure, whether it be the giant military governmental complex, the family, the universities, or simply the "status quo." His Critical Philosophy has apparent roots in the Frankfurt School of Social Research and in the early Marxist revisionists like Rosa Luxemburg and Karl Kautsky, all of which philosophical thinking is anti-authoritarian. In fact, the main point of Feuerbach's *Essence of Christianity* is an attempt to demythologize all authoritarian structures by centering the attack against the belief in a real God and in the institutionalized structures that defend such a belief.

Furthermore, ethicians and political scientists over the centuries have been vague in their treatment of the notion of authority. The old scholastic textbooks referred to authority as the "form" of society; the newer ones omitted the point altogether. Even Professor Carl J. Friedrich's volume in the "Nomos" series (1958) entitled "Authority" did not venture further back with any depth beyond the post-Reformation era. The "Syntopicon", a nugget of philosophical concepts in the tradition of the West, has no special topic on "authority." This is strange in the light of what has happened. Yet, now as the crisis emerges more dangerously, there are signs of life reappearing from the long hibernation. Professor Friedrich himself has written a new book on authority soon to appear from the Oxford Press. And, Professor De George, one of the contributors to this volume, is working on a new book on this subject. Thus, it is hoped that the appropriateness of this volume will be recognized and that it will have an enzymatic function in so necessary a philosophical enterprise.

On the other hand, attacks against authority are coming at us from all sides – from the media, the journalists and by such academicians as Kenneth Megill, Robert Paul Wolff, Juergen Habermas, Hans Kueng and, of course, Marcuse. But the anti-authoritarians have had it too easy. No one likes authority unless he possesses it. It offends the long line of libertarian thinking that built up the ego of the young and the "do your own thing" well-wishers. Due to the ingenuous abolition of authority and the sleight-of-hand maneuvers of re-entry in the form of structural anarchy and participatory democracy, the thoughtful person becomes confused having forgotten the still valid dichotomy between authority and anarchy. So the authoritarians for their part have had a hard time of it in a milieu that denies or defies distinctions. Anyone committed to authority is considered a conservative in the pejorative sense, or perhaps a fascist, or at least unwilling to change in an inevitably changing world.

But, nonetheless, there will be authority, and if it could be otherwise, there would be no community at all. And to deny this historical and sociological fact is to play a role that, if multiplied, is the usual cause for dictators being able to take over.

Still the problem connected with the philosophical idea of authority is complex and probably has not been solved within the pages of this volume. Part of the complexity is that authority is not just a philosophical notion but can only adequately be dealt with on the metaphysical level. And here I use the term metaphysical to refer to a way of understanding those very real phenomena in reality that cannot be properly handled by the functions of logical analysis nor the measurements of empiricism. This is not to say that these sources cannot be recourceful in the investigation. It is merely to stress the *locus* of any philosophical problem related to persons, their wills and their community. One of the essays included in this volume does attempt to analyze authority in terms of modern logic. How successful the attempt by Professor Bochenski has been, will be up to the judgment of the reader.

Another point that should be kept in mind throughout any discussion of authority is the new realization of change in society. Hegel has bequeathed this notion to all subsequent thinkers; Marx and the Marxists have corroborated his insight. Technology, evolution, historical developments in political emancipation are further abettors to the thesis. Anyone who stands against the whirling changes of contemporary life hoping for a cyclic return to more serene times is no real defender of the valid theoretical and practical understanding of authority. The old definitions in the light of this acceleration of social change are as inadequate in their static forms as many of the new are in their disdain for tradition.

This volume should prove interesting, then, for serious philosophers of anthropology, sociology and political science. The contributors are all philosophers in the sense that they are metaphilosophers or metaphysicians. They represent various backgrounds and commitments; their only common interest, perhaps, is their realization of the importance of authority as a topic to be discussed today. Still, from the content of the essays, one could further aver that the writers are both realists and even metaphysicians in the wide sense of those terms. It will be up to the reader to discern any common thematic running through the independent research that has entered into the compilation. If such be the case then the purpose of the original proposal and the furtherance of the debate will have been accomplished.

In this introduction, I simply want to say that it was with great sorrow that the editor learned of the death in November 1972 of Professor John Wild, one of our contributors. Although he had suffered a prior stroke he was excited about this topic of authority and exerted his keen mind to finish his excellent article. Out of deep respect for his long years in the lecture hall and the many students whom he inspired and encouraged, we have dedicated this volume to his memory.

In the front of the book, a brief autobiographical sketch of our contributors has been published. However, it is perhaps interesting for me to add to that *curriculum vitae* some of the reasons why I asked these philosophers to contribute. Professor Bochenski is a versatile philosopher who is a specialist not only in Thomistic thought but in the history of logical systems. In recent years he has written on the history of European contemporary philosophy and has made Marxism one of his principal interests. From his long experience of life in Poland, Germany, Italy and Switzerland and from his experience with graduate students over the years, his insights into the notion of authority through mathematical logic bring a new dimension to the whole discussion.

Although I have never met Professor Davis personally, his ability as a philosopher came to my attention some years ago when I read his monograph on *The Free Will*. It seemed that one who had grasped the metaphysical implications of will theory as manifested in that volume, would have something valuable to contribute on a topic so closely related. It seems to me that Professor Davis has set forth his own reflections on authority that will stimulate thought about the problem even among those who may not agree with his analysis.

Karl Rahner is undoubtedly the leading Catholic theologian in the world today. His ability to both retain the diversity and overcome it in the form-matter relations pervading the universe has given new insights to individual thinkers in every field of philosophy. From his early work entitled *Geist in Welt* to his prominent role in Vatican Council II, one perceives his ability to incorporate insights from Hegel and Heidegger into the *philosophia perennis* and, indeed, he does this again in his article here about the authority within the Church.

Bernard Lonergan is also a professor of theology, yet he is perhaps most remembered because of his philosophical treatise entitled *Insight* which despite its length and profundity, soon had so great an influence among students that one could almost say that today there is a Lonergan school. Father Lonergan's greatest contribution seems to have been made in the area of methodology and he brings that flavor to his discussion of authority.

Professor De George has become a specialist in Marxist philosophy and has published several books in this area. In studying Soviet ethics he seems to have become interested in the relation of the human person to the state. As a result most recently he has been working on a new book about authority soon to appear. Here in his contribution we have an opportunity to see in a more succinct way what he thinks authority is all about.

My own interest in the subject of authority is both personal and professional. After doing much research about will theory since my doctoral studies, the problem soon led into reflections about the true meaning of authority. It is strange, too, how many of the contributors including myself have been independent students of Marxism. Thus, professors Bochenski, Rahner, De George, and myself have perhaps been given a thrust in this direction by the virtue of the dialectic we encountered in Marxist studies between the individual person and the dictates of the party. In my own case, especially, this thrust was made because of the seeming Marxist denial of any constant human nature and the need to define man solely in relation to the social organism.

Just as the great fear of anti-authoritarians has been about the limiting of authority, so one common theme that runs through these analyses emphasizes this point, but with this difference, namely there is always the hope of salvaging authority itself. It is up to the reader to try to discern the truth enunciated partially at least in each of these essays, keeping in mind, of course, that any of us in our human philosophical speculations is also limited.

The Editor

AUTHORITY

John Wild

Before we can properly compare different attitudes towards authority, we must have a clear understanding of the meaning of this very obscure and inclusive term. What do we mean by an authority in general usage? What is its nature and how does it function? What are its valid forms, and how do these become corrupt and perverted? I shall begin by considering these fundamental questions and suggesting a way of answering them which seems to me to be defensible. Then, in in the light of this answer, I shall conclude with a brief analysis of the more special forms of authority and how they fit into a more general view.

An authority, of course, is a person whose knowledge or character, or both, brings him so close to a recognized value as to call forth the respect of others and to enable him to speak and to act for them. If he says one thing and does another, he is divided against himself and cannot be a single authority. The word has a multitude of varying meanings of which each one is single when unambiguously expressed. In past times this single, positive sense has played an influential and even predominant role. Thus it is said of Our Lord in the Gospels that he spoke as one with authority, and not as the scribes; that is, as one possessing special knowledge and special virtues deserving of special attention and respect. In the field of science and theoretical truth in general we speak of exceptionally learned men as "authorities" in their respective fields though this is a special, not the general meaning. Thus we refer, say to Einstein, as an "authority" in the field of theoretical physics.

But if we reflect on current usage, we cannot help but be impressed by certain pejorative senses which have come to the fore. The term "authoritarian," for example, is one of reproach, standing for an attitude of "unquestioning" obedience rather than "individual freedom of judgement and action." Most courses in *Ethics*, as they used to be given in our Colleges and Universities, began with a discussion of this sort of "authoritarianism," the blind acceptance of moral opinions without defensible reasons on the sole basis of custom. Such a moral view was held to be inexcusably naive. Hence, it was passed over very rapidly, so that more time could be spent on other views more worthy of attention.

This pejorative usage of words connected with authority is now very widespread. It has even affected the word "authority" itself, which has now fallen into that neglect which is often the fate of words regarded as antiquarian, referring to social structures and attitudes now thought to be definitely passé. On a subject like "sovereignty," for example, there is a wide array of technical literature in our libraries. But treatises on authority are definitely scarce. This fact is strange. Why is it so? I think that it is derived from certain attitudes of the liberal mind. Two, especially, are worthy of attention, both being derived from a common, moral prejudice, that freedom is easy and natural.

The first of these is the ever-present liberal tendency to identify liberty with license, doing as you please, requiring no effort. If this is so, any readiness to follow an alien authority, in thought or action, must be diagnosed as a loss of autonomy, which is very evil. Each free man must think for himself and make his own choices. "To think for himself" is here interpreted as brooding over one's own desires. To make his own choices means to do what one would do anyway. To be directed by an external authority is to sacrifice liberty. From this point of view, the liberal grudgingly admits that the immature child, or backward nation may not yet be capable of self-government (first pps. of Mill, *On Liberty*). For those in such sub-human states, external control or benevolent dictatorship is justified insofar as it aims at its own destruction. The more we advance towards civilization, the less authority we need. It can be actually justified only in sub-normal circumstances, *faute de mieux*. The goal of all intelligent aspiration is a condition of anarchy, in which each man decides for himself without the aid of tradition and authority of any kind. This goal will never be perfectly achieved. Insanity and immaturity will always be with us. But it can be asymptotically approximated. Virtue is not artificially contrived. It is simple and natural. Human progress is equivalent to the gradual elimination of authority. This view is extraordinarily influential at the present time. It is spread as far as the liberal mind itself.

This first attitude toward freedom is strongly reinforced by a second attitude, a certain conception of the nature of authority which is often defended by conservative writers, apparently opposed to liberalism. According to this conception, authority is taken to be an ungrounded power of issuing commands, residing in a single person, or in a group of persons. Thus Yves Simon defines authority as: "an active power residing in a person and exercised through a command ... to be taken as a rule of conduct by the free will of another person," lacking the time or opportunity to think it through for himself. (*Nature and Functions of Authority*, p. 7). Simon is evidently thinking primarily of politics and political power, a clear manifestation of authority which touches the life of everyone. As we shall see, his definition fails to express accurately the nature of this complex structure. No man is born free by nature. We must think anxiously and deliberate about our freedom. It is never given by nature but is always contrived. We lose our freedom by natural relapses. We never gain it in this way, but rather by that method we call authority. It is fair to say, I believe, that without the instruments of authority, freedom would never be a common possession of a group or a nation. It would rather be restricted to a few outstanding individuals.

But there are other situations, involving authority, to which the bipolar definition in terms of power and command, does not fit at all. Thus a historian of Greece may say that Thucydides is his authority for a certain interpretation of events at the beginning of the Peloponnesian War. This is certainly not a simple bipolar situation in which someone with power is giving commands to others. Thucydides witnessed certain events, and analyzed them with such penetration that he is able to guide later historians towards the truth. The situation is not dyadic, but rather triadic. There is truth to be conveyed, and those ready and able to receive it. The authority is he who occupies a middle position, and exercises a mediating function, conveying the truth to free minds not in a position directly to apprehend it for themselves. There is no question of giving commands. Thucydides is long dead, and wrote his history in seclusion, after losing his naval command.

A similar analysis will apply to cases of the exercise of what we may call intellectual or theoretical authority. Einstein, it is true, possesses a certain power over the free minds of those interested in the structure of the physical world. But this power is grounded in his disciplined intelligence and ultimately on the knowledge of physical structure which this has enabled him to attain. Here again we have a triadic situation: authentic truth and free minds eager to receive it. The authority is a third, mediating factor, a person of exceptional intelligence and discipline, standing closer to the truth, who is, therefore, in a position to exercise a mediating function, bringing this value of truth to others who are properly prepared.

A similar analysis applies to another special meaning, the legal sense of authority. The last will of a dying man is said to have authority because it expresses his last wishes, and is, therefore, able to mediate between the free minds of the living and the value, the will of the man now dead. Here the value to be conveyed is the will of one no longer able to speak or to act for himself. The authority transmits this will to the minds of others still able to act. In a similar manner, the agent for one in some way incapacitated, or physically remote, is said to have complete legal authority, if he has been duly authorized by the absent person to transact business without limitation in his behalf. Here, the mediating function is exceptionally clear. It is always a bridge between a remote or hidden value of some sort, and free minds prepared to receive it. Therefore, if it is to function adequately, two conditions must be met.

In the first place, the authority must be adequately grounded in the value to be transmitted. The historical authority must have actually witnessed the events, and must have understood them to some degree of clarity. The scientific authority must possess knowledge authentically grounded in the structure of things. The legal authority must know and express the will of the first agent. His mediating acts must be duly authorized by this first agent, and must accurately express his will. Any genuine authority must have some peculiar access to the value it is conveying; it must be duly authorized and grounded. Otherwise, it will have nothing of real value to transmit.

In the second place, a genuine authority must be able to transmit the value of truth, goodness, or beauty, whatever it may be, to free minds by rational persuasion. This is why all authority is personal. Only a person with rational intelligence and the freedom derived from this intelligence can freely communicate values to other persons without jeopardizing their freedom. Without authority there can be no freedom; nor any being such as the person. One sub-cognitive being may act on another by first acting on a third, as the sun, by holding one planet in its orbit may introduce perturbations in the orbit of another. But it is only metaphorically that we can say any one planet has an authoritative effect on another. There is no authority; merely the rule of the greater force.

By means of our technology, human beings may impress the force of their wills upon the sub-cognitive powers of nature. But there is no authority here. Such powers respond automatically as their natures direct, not by any free recognition of authority. Those with so-called sovereign power may frighten children or adult crowds into blind submission by displays of physical force. By technological devices, they may condition them, while young, into automatic modes of response, and may dream of controlling them, like the sub-intelligent forces of nature, but only with the sacrifice of freedom and intelligence on the part of those thus controlled. We may lose social freedom in this way; we may never gain it. Such sub-rational communication of sovereign power by dictate and command is now often confused with authority. But this usage is not borne out by our analysis. It is a misuse of the word "authority," which simply does not apply to the examples we have given.

Thucydides has no sovereign power over us. He cannot condition us. Rational persuasion alone is at his disposal. And yet he may be an authority. Einstein has no police at his beck and call. He issues no pure commands. Yet he also may be an authority. An agent armed with legal authority to negotiate who armed himself with physical weapons and proceeded to make his points by a show of daggers and knives would not only make himself ludicrous, but would soon lose all the authority he had ever possessed. Genuine authority, it would seem, has nothing to do with sheer, physical force, in the instances we have been studying. It is not a dyadic relation in which someone exerts mere power over others. This relation belongs to sub-human nature where authority, in the proper sense, does not appear.

Authority is rather a triadic, not a dyadic relation. One term of this triadic relation is a real value of some kind, capable of being understood. The other two terms are free and rational agents. One of these, the authority, occupies a mediating position between the two. On the one hand, he must possess a peculiar closeness to the value in question – an essential ground of his authority. On the other, he must be able to communicate the value by rational persuasion to other free minds – the third term of the triadic relation. These free persons come to follow the value from which they are widely separated by space, time, or ignorance. But they must be also prepared by attitude and discipline to receive it. At the very least they must be interested. They must know enough to be able to recognize the value when it is transmitted, to prize it, and to respect the authority through whom they received it. Such a situation, when it arises, or when it is closely approximated, is referred to by the word "authority."

This word (authority) may then be defined as: a person having some special access to a real value which he is able to transmit to other free minds, prepared to receive it with discipline and respectful attention, while it is still not yet fully actualized. In this sense, authority must be recognized as an indispensable condition for the free and relatively rapid communication concerning personal values between free persons. Without authority, mass conditioning, of course, would still be possible. Animal life might still proceed, but a free society of free persons would be impossible. Without respect for the authority of those who already know something, no one would listen to another, and education could no longer proceed. Authority grounded in the authentic knowledge of what is really so, and in the respect of those sufficiently trained to receive it, is the bulwark of democratic society.

But here we must face an important objection. It may be said, that while our choice of examples has been fairly wide, it has not been wide enough. It is still a biased choice, heavily loaded in favor of intellectual instances of intellectual authority. So we have emerged with a theory that is onesidedly rationalistic and idealistic – a philosopher's dream of what authority might be in an ivory tower College, but remote from the actual facts of life, especially of political life, a real dimension of human existence. Wherever two or more people are found to be acting together, this dimension is found. What are at stake here are not values that have ever been realized before. As in the case of revolutionary action, these are values being realized for the first time with no precedent. Thus there is nothing for anyone to familiarize himself with, nothing for anyone to transmit. The hard facts of cooperative life simply do not fit into your scheme. The authority of office in a great, modern state has nothing to do with special access to values already realized of an intellectual kind. This office is purely an instrument of power, for the sake of values not yet achieved. This power is sovereign and, therefore, not grounded on anything not itself. Values are not transmitted but *made* by the political power, through its exercise of sovereignty.

What the values are to be is a matter of choice. If they are determined by those in power and imposed on the people, this is tyranny though possibly of a benevolent sort. To avoid this, we have the bill of rights, which weakens government, lessens the danger of mass tyranny, and, so far as possible, enables everyone to do as he likes, the real meaning of human freedom. Such is the very influential, so-called liberal view of political authority. It certainly does not fit our scheme.

According to this theory, authority involves only two factors not three – the people and the govermental power they establish. Authority is this sovereign power, pure and simple. On the whole, such authority should be weakened. The more progress we make politically, the less authority we shall need.

Now let us examine this liberal objection. Is it sound? In attempting to work out an answer, we must notice one significant fact. If this analysis is correct, we must conclude that what we have called "political authority" is entirely different from the intellectual and legal types we have been studying. They possess the same triadic structure that has now become familiar to us. Each of these authorities has a responsibility not to one alone but to two divergent factors, the real value he is transmitting and the free minds to whom he is transmitting it. A failure in either respect, but especially in the first, will eventually corrupt the authority. But now we are asked to conclude that the most common type of authority, as widespread as cooperative life itself, that which is political, is completely different in character. It is not basically grounded on any real value which it has the duty to transmit. It is rather an ungrounded power. Indeed, its function is not transmissive at all, but rather constructive and formative, by the issuing of commands and decrees to be carried out by the use of force, or the threat of force. Hence authority cannot be regarded as distinctively personal. There is nothing distinctively personal about power as such. It will be rather very closely allied to those bipolar systems of sub-human nature in which one center of balanced forces exercises dominance over the rest.

If this is so, the word "authority" will be altogether ambiguous and equivocal, used in two utterly divergent senses having no basic structure in common. In pointing to two unrelated meanings rather than to one, our language will be fundamentally mistaken. Of course, this may be true. No language is infallible. But in spite of inexactitude which we ignore at our peril, there is a certain wisdom which pertains to this common speech which also needs recognition. Before concluding that it has made an obvious blunder, we should, at least, give the matter some serious attention. So let us examine this analysis of authority as power, and of politics as power politics. Is this analysis sound? Let us begin by asking why it is that in all communities so far known, we find political authority established. Moral disputes constantly arise. And for settling them, those capable of arbitrating judgements are set up in power. Why is this necessary?

The answer, I think, is clear. Human life cannot be lived without the assistance of other persons cooperating together in the achievement of a common good including the good of each one. The other social animals have been endowed by nature with specific instincts which automatically attain such ends. Man has not been so endowed. In place of such tendencies, he has been granted the faculty of intelligence by which he can understand something of himself and of the world in which he lives, and that of free action by which he can guide himself by such knowledge. Some insight into the nature of the end of man, and of those principles of natural law which must be followed if this end is to be attained, is accessible to all men, and may be set up as a standard to adjudicate disputes by the group authority.

This must be grounded in a sound practical knowledge of the main lines of social policy along which group action is to be directed to achieve the common good. The exercise of undirected power, pure power, can lead only to confusion and disaster. Also, the group authority must be capable of analyzing the flux of situations, of making quick decisions, and of calling forth concerted action to meet crises without delay. This function cannot be performed without special abilities and special training. Everyone in the community, if there is one, cannot take an equal share. The very essence of social life lies in the division of labor. If all citizens were under a constant call to participate in group deliberations concerning common policy, they would be distracted from necessary tasks which would be neglected. Furthermore, group deliberations of this kind are apt to be protracted and cumbersome. By the time a decision has been reached, the crisis would be over, and nothing would have been done. Certain individuals must be chosen to exercise these crucial functions for the common good. There is no other way. Persons with political authority must direct group action. Does this analysis meet the requirements of our theory of authority? I think that it does.

All authority involves the transmission of some value to free peoples.

Of course, the nature of the authority will vary with the nature of the value to be transmitted. In the case of intellectual values, the truth must be clearly known to the authority, and conveyed without distortion by persuasion. But practical attitudes are also involved, for the aspiration to truth cannot be fulfilled unless deeds are actually done. Those who are about to learn must already possess a respect for knowledge, and must be ready to listen. Otherwise nothing can be conveyed. The common goods for which we strive do not yet actually exist. They must be brought into actual being from their state of potency by cooperative action, ordered by authority.

As a rational authority inspires respect, so a practical authority inspires active obedience. But understanding is also presupposed. Though not actually present, the value to be attained must be intentionally present before the mind of the guiding authority as well as the minds of all the active agents. Men will not exert themselves to achieve what they do not understand. In each case, there is a value to be conveyed to free persons prepared to receive it. The authority performs a mediating function. His primary responsibility is to achieve a position of intimate closeness to the real value. His second duty is then to communicate it by thought and action to free minds without the loss of their freedom. Unless the value transmitted is really authorized and authentic, his exercise of authority is in vain. Hence his first responsibility is to make sure that the value in question is genuine. Even though no one will listen to a thinker, it is still his duty to communicate what he knows to be true. Even though no one at the time agrees with him, it is the duty of a statesman to struggle for the right. This is the only effective remedy against tyranny, for, as we now know, mass tyranny is more terrible than the tyranny of a few.

But while secondary and derivative, the duty to communicate is absolutely essential. An authority which cannot convey what it knows to be authorized is only potential at best. Hence it must be constantly on guard against that alienation from the people to which it is always susceptible. The most tragic state of a culture is to lack all authority. But next after this is the alienation of a culture from its authorities, which rapidly leads to the first. Only the person can be an authority, and to exercise this onerous function requires great personal gifts and sacrificial zeal. Such persons are only rarely given, and the span of a lifetime is very brief. They are apt to be succeeded by lesser men, who are unequal to the task and allow themselves to become alienated from those they are supposed to guide.

This sequence of events has been thoroughly studied by Toynbee in his study of history as the degeneration of what he calls a *creative minority* into a *dominant minority*. This is essentially the alienation of a people from its authorities. Living communication between extraordinary minds and the masses is lost. Authority is no longer clearly understood. Instead of guiding, it commands, and appears as something grim, remote, and formidable. On the part of the people, sacrificial zeal in the pursuit of great, overarching purposes is replaced by mechanical imitation (mimesis). Finally, all authority is lost, and the culture breaks down into a chaos of warring fragments which is inevitably resolved by the establishment of mass tyranny, the presumed end of civilization. This tragic sequence has been repeated again and again in the history of world civilizations. Our Western culture is now threatened with it. Is there any remedy against that failure of authority which is its crucial, initiating phase? I believe that there is.

It is called "tradition." Without it, no human authority can be kept alive in and through the flux of generations. It stands like a rugged island resisting the continuous flow of time. By means of it, the guiding insight and appeal of classic authorities are maintained and transmitted to successive generations which are kept in a state of readiness for new authorities to come. In desolate periods, when great leaders are lacking, delicate shades of meaning and emphasis are lost but the essence remains, as in the case of the negative dynamism of the Hegelian tradition, which supported Marx. Including not only the exceptional contributions of great men, but also the humbler work of lesser figures, it exercises a strange appeal to the devotion of free minds, whatever their degree of natural talent. Preserving not only the insight but also the grace and charm of classic authorities, it mitigates that austerity and remoteness into which average authority is ever apt to fall. At every level of social activity, *tradition* is the greatest force that preserves and incites true authority, mediating between exceptional, authentic insights of the past and free minds of the present.

This analysis has been all too brief. I think, however, that it may have been sufficient to show the falsity of a very widespread conception of authority. It is not the nature of genuine authority merely to issue orders and commands to a subservient mass. This is a typical debasement, a primitive mode. Authority has as many diverse types as there are social values to be achieved by cooperative action. But the term is not equivocal. All of these types share a common triadic structure. There is always some genuine value or disvalue which can be understood by free minds. Authority stands in the middle, exercising a mediating function between the two, bringing the value to those prepared by tradition to receive it by rational persuasion and practical guidance.

This practical guidance is no exception to our triadic structural rule, which is grounded on an actual value to be achieved by common action. Its function is to bring such a value to free agents by offering that directing, mediating guidance without which no practical goal can be attained except by accident. But the command, or imperative is not categorical. It is hypothetical in character. If such and such a value is to be rationally aimed at and achieved, such and such must be done. To think of such authority as a source of mere power, issuing categorical commands, with no ground, is to misunderstand its mediating character. It does not only give orders; it gives grounded orders, for the sake of some understandable goal. It exercises no command *over* subservient subjects; it rather gives hypothetical commands *for* free agents committed already to a cooperative enterprise.

Let us now attempt briefly to apply the results of our analysis to what in our Western tradition is the supreme level of all authority, that which we call "religious." We are certainly confronted here with the triadic structure that has now become familiar. On the one hand, we have the ultimate goodness of God, Himself; on the other hand, the mass of mankind fallen into sin, but still free, and struggling to preserve their freedom. The task of religious authority is to act as a mediating link bringing the one to the other without the use of force, and the loss of human freedom which brute force would imply. At the present time this communication is subject to two extreme distortions. The first is an inadequate emphasis on transcendence which is interpreted in terms of force alone with less attention paid to freedom and the inner life of the divine. The second is a consequence of this as it affects human communication. When transcendence is interpreted in terms of force alone, existing before transcendence, it becomes not freedom, but a kind of slavery, a weakness of human freedom. Any correction of this lack must imply an interest in the inner life, where alone freedom becomes visible, and an interest in freedom itself and its various kinds, such as was found in existential philosophy. Indeed, it may be said, that for this time, freedom became almost an obsession, as it may absorb the major energies of creative thought in the future.

Since God is transcendent, and since divine values are inaccessible to the unaided human faculties, the mediation must be initiated and sustained by God Himself incarnate. Thus the supreme, religious authority is the person of Christ, both man and God, the mediator *par excellence*, who spoke as one *with authority*. In exercising this mediating function, he showed us the way in which all genuine, earthly authority of lesser kind and degree should be exercised.

It is clear that this authority is firmly grounded in the eternal values he is conveying, for He and the Father are one and the same. So far as possible, he tries to focus the attention of the listeners away from Himself on the Divine Truth he is transmitting. It is not I who speak but the Father who speaks *through* me. Genuine authority is always vicarious and self-effacing; it both is and is not the ultimate standard. This standard does not enslave mankind in any way: it always liberates. You shall know the truth and the truth shall make you free. Anything that will limit this authority in any way, or will restrict its mode of human reception to certain set forms will interfere with it.

Living in the closest proximity with the Divine Agency he is conveying, he moves with a free and easy grace among the multitudes of men. Ceaselessly devoting himself to this general purpose, making himself accessible to the humblest, unsparing of his time and energy, He conveys his message by thought and word and deed, never endangering its unity. Scorning the use of physical force, he maintains an unswerving respect for the personal freedom of those with whom he speaks On the one hand, unlimited action, on the other hand, unrestricted attention. So far does this lack of restraint on human freedom go that he finally allows himself to be betrayed by one of his own disciples who freely decides against him. He seems to be interested not in passive subservience, but rather in free devotion. Here also is a pattern which, to some degree at least, has been approximated by the greatest human authorities, such as Socrates, for example.

Here we find our familiar, triadic structure, the value itself, the free persons who are to achieve or to realize it, and the authority through whom it is to be achieved. The breakdown of this tripartite structure follows the identification of the third, mediating factor (authority) with one of the other two (either the divine, or the human). In the first place, the awareness of authority is inadequately discriminated against the divine, and then against the human. The consciousness of authority as a third independent factor is absent. We shall now take up these two diseases in the order which has been given (1) the lack of the divine, and (2) the lack of the human, as well as combinations of the two acting together, which fall under this second (2) heading. These degradations of authority do not correspond exactly to the precise divisions between sects. They are to be found within all such divisions, where the notion of authority is to be found.

Thus under (1) what we may call "the traditional, orthodox conception of authority" presents us with the picture of a movement of authority away from its subjective pole, and towards identification of itself with its ground. Here we find an authority forgetting its responsibilities for the illumination of free persons, and moving away from them into a more forbidding remoteness, towards a final confusion of itself with its own, objective ground. Instead of being illumined and instructed, like free men, her communicants rather give the impression of being ordered and commanded, like human subjects, browbeaten and anathematized, regularized and regimented. This is authority *over* not authority *for*. There is too great a distance between the authority and its beneficiaries. One wonders whether the authority is for them, or they are for the authority.

But as the authority recedes farther from the subjective pole, it tries to approximate more closely to the objective pole, until this is actually confused with itself. In reading orthodox accounts of authority from different sects, one wonders whether the Church transmits a deposit of Faith, because it is really true, or, whether it is really true because the Church authority transmits it, and has oracularly pronounced it to be true. We seem to be confronted here with an authority which has abandoned its mediating function, and has mistakenly identified itself with the authentic values it is attempting to convey, like a teacher who might confuse himself with the truth he is trying to teach. In the religious sphere, this presents us with the familiar picture of a degraded political authority which has collapsed, into the all too familiar dyadic structure of tyrannical power giving arbitrary commands to inert subjects.

Unorthodox, or making use of the term in a very general sense, Protestant, versions of authority seem, contrary to the orthodox view, to identify themselves with their subjective or human pole, and to be gradually losing touch with their primary, objective ground. This is authority passing away or coming to an end. So the word "authority" now comes to mean, not "authority" in the proper sense of this word, but rather the need for some authority. It is in close touch with the minds of its members and with modern currents of secular thought. But even in its own view, it seems remote from its primary source, and hesitant as to its ground. In its more liberal versions, this is openly expressed. In those which are more traditional, it is manifested less directly by a compensatory dogmatism. Its rejection of certain sacramental traditions, and of many other, living traditions of religious faith and life has further weakened the claim of this degraded mode of religious "authority" to have anything of any special importance to communicate.

Having cut themselves off from living traditions bearing authority, they claim to be only members of fine people, gathered together for a worthy purpose; but having nothing of special importance to communicate. Such groups may hope to be granted some authority at some time. But barring extraordinary events in the future, they do not claim to have it now. They are like a number of ordinary men meeting together for the purpose of studying mathematics, but with no special closeness to the subject gained either through the possession of exceptional texts, or through concentrated study. Such a group might elect officers with administrative authority, empowered to call meetings, and to find teachers who might know something about the subject; but they would have no specifically mathematical authority.

In this way, unorthodox groups, self-formed and self-organized, would seem to have nothing peculiarly religious to transmit, no specially religious authority. Their history shows us the typical sequence which tends to occur when an authority isolates itself from its ground. Such an authority becomes groundless and therefore, arbitrary. This encourages dissidence and rebellion on the part of subordinate groups which can separate themselves from the main body even farther and set up their own opposed authorities, with even less to transmit. The sequence finally ends in a chaos of eager and well-meaning groups with no authority at all.

These are the two bipolar extremes which have eliminated the triadic structure of mediating authority between man and God. Authority either takes on the divine element at the expense of the human and becomes unduly rigorous and remote, or it takes on the human element at the expense of the divine and loses its distinctive properties. Changes of this sort have happened in the long and tortuous history of the notion "authority." In this history, it has no doubt oscillated between a greater emphasis on the divine (in orthodoxy) and a greater emphasis on the human (heterodoxy). In spite of the greater emphasis on one factor at the expense of the other, there are in all cases two factors always present. There is always *something* of the divine and *something* of the human really present, which is why we have referred to both views as "bipolar." Each view holds within it something radically other than itself, the human and something different, the divine. We have not as yet come to the radical end of this sceptical trend. It does not end in bipolarity, but in mono-polarity, the end of all otherness.

Suppose that we are willing to take the last step in drawing our sceptical conclusion. Then we shall not be content with attenuating the divine element in human experience. We shall be willing to go to the last degree in *eliminating* it. Then in our first step towards an exaggeration of authority, in emphasizing its divine ground, and in minimizing its human component, we shall not merely attenuate but we shall eliminate it altogether. This will leave us with no human experience, with nothing at all. Either something of man remains or absolute scepticism, nothing at all. And similarly with the next step towards heterodoxy, as we called it. We shall no longer be content to attenuate the divine. We shall simply eliminate it altogether. This will not leave us with nothing (scepticism) but with human experience (the human). The divine, now, what is it, as has recently been maintained, if not human imagination? Here is man at last finally alone. Nothing in our experience can be found, without some human ground. In our human experience there is no radical otherness. All is on the same fundamental level. There is really no bi-polarity. All is mono-polar in its basic ground. Men may talk together. But never with anything or anyone else, though such may be imagined.

It is against this mono-polar, humanly grounded scepticism that what we have called proper "authority" must wage its struggle today. Sweeping aside the minor complications of controversy, we state the issue briefly as a struggle for otherness. Where, in the total range of our human experience, is genuine otherness to be found? Where is that which is non-human to be sought for and explored? Where is that which cannot be explained as a human imagining nor any mere combination of human acts or works? Religion is the outstanding candidate for such non-human status. Can it be properly defended as such? But here we must remember the arguments of philosophical idealism which have shown how easy it is to construct a concept for every item of given experience and to reduce all concepts to their human ground. The strongest statement, perhaps, of this point of view is to be found in Hegel. Can it be answered? Where, if anywhere, is the non-conceptual given to us? Is it in pleasure and sense experience? Is the non-human to be found at the very heart of our human experience? A subtle statement of the case that can be made out for this has been formulated by the French philosopher, Levinas, in his great book *Totality and Infinity*. We may expect further elaborations of this case in the near future. Do we touch the non-conceptual in the inner life of man as it is directly lived by him? And after the last conceptual judgements have been made? This question has now been asked, and needs to be further examined.

Human works, i.e., works of art and writings which he has authorized result from his labors and remain after him as the objects of our concepts and the objective reality we associate with him. But they fall into the hands of others, who interpret them, so that, as we say, they live a life of their own, often quite alien to the intentions of their authors. Something is omitted here – the intention itself as lived. As over against objective judgements on the admittedly objective facts, there seems to be appeal. As formulated by Hegel they constitute the judgement of history on itself – *Die Weltgeschichte ist die Weltgericht*, and when all the judgements have been adequately fitted together, there can be no appeal to anything other. But if inner life exists as an independent entity, some sort of an appeal to this may be made. Does this appeal exist? Or does it not? This is at least one question that surely will be asked.

Other questions concerning human otherness are bound to be raised. Does the horizon of the Divine or Infinite being open up new, and non-human perspectives on the existence of man? Can these horizons of otherness be properly defended? Remembering the intentional character of human experience, can we say that this experience gives us views of the non-human as well as the human? If so, what light does this shed on the nature of such experience? Can it be said, at least, that it renders it more open and flexible than before? Can the other of X be interpreted as the logical opposite or negation of X in the Hegelian manner? If the Divine Other can be properly defended, does this shed any light on the nature of the human other? Does this notion fall within the limits of any prescribed category? If not, how then is the human other related to the Divine, a question not raised by Levinas?

If in my experience I am confronted with something radically different from myself, does this not have ethical implications for me? If I have not been radically faced with this question, have I ever really faced the questions of ethics? What, for example, shall I do with one who is utterly strange and alien to me? Can I use violence against him? Can I kill? Does not my willingness to converse with him suggest the answer? Does this not imply an ethics of hospitality, hardly even conceived before? Am I to answer it, or am I not? Is this not an ethical question underlying all the rest? Has it ever been actually faced? Since logic and ontology require giving answers of some kind, does this not clearly indicate the priority of ethics over the other philosophical disciplines, and the evident fact that its questions are raised and answered before theirs?

If the notions of self and other are equally primordial, must we not then regard the ways in which self has predominated over other throughout our Western history as clearcut manifestations of egotism? Is it not time, for example, that someone at least *leaned* towards a nonself-centered system of ethics? It has become habitual for us to regard the other as really a self in his own right. But is it not equally correct to regard the self also as an other? Should it not be good usage for him to inquire what sort of an other am I? And do I contain an other in myself? And how do I treat this other in me?

DIALECTIC OF AUTHORITY*

Bernard Lonergan

Authority is legitimate power. The dialectic will emerge from a reflection on power and legitimacy.

The source of power is cooperation. Cooperation is twofold. There is cooperation down the ages. There is cooperation at any given place and time.

Without cooperation down the ages human life today would not differ from that of the most primitive tribe. It would be not merely Preaurignacian, as the celebrated ethologist, Konrad Lorenz, has been repeating to students, but would resemble that of the isolated people recently discovered in the forest rain-country in the Philippines. Power today results from all the achievements of the past that have been accumulated, developed, integrated. Any present is powerful in the measure that past achievement lives on in it.

Besides the cooperation that extends down the ages, there is the cooperation that is going on here and now. The group can do so much that the individual cannot do. The group of groups is so much more efficient than the isolated group. Grouping groups is a device that can be reapplied again and again and, with each reapplication that results in an organic whole, power is multiplied.

As the source of power is cooperation, so the carrier of power is the community. By a community is not meant a number of people within a frontier. Community means people with a common field of experience, with a common or at least complementary way of understanding people and things, with common judgements and common aims. Without a common field of experience people are out of touch. Without a common way of understanding, they will misunderstand one another, grow suspicious, distrustful, hostile, violent. Without common judgements they will live in different worlds, and without common aims they will

---

* © Copyright 1973 by Bernard Lonergan.

work at cross-purposes. Such, then, is community, and as it is community that hands on the discoveries and inventions of the past and, as well cooperates in the present, so it is community that is the carrier of power.

The exercise of power is twofold. For men live in two worlds. From infancy they live in a world of immediacy, a world revealed by sense and alive with feeling. Gradually they move into a world mediated by meaning and motivated by values. In this adult world the raw materials are indeed the world of immediacy. But by speech one asks when and where, what and why, what for and how often. Answers cumulatively extrapolate from what is near to what is ever further away, from the present to one's own and to others' memories of the past and anticipations of the future, from what is or was actual to the possible, the probable, the fictitious, the ideal, the normative.

As exercised within the world mediated by meaning and motivated by values, power resides in the word of authority. It is that word that brings the achievements of the past into the present; it is that word that organizes and directs the whole hierarchy of cooperating groups in the present; it is that word that distributes the fruits of cooperation among the cooperating members; it is that word that bans from social intercourse those that would disrupt the cooperating society. In brief, the word of authority is the current actuality of the power generated by past development and contemporary cooperation.

To a great extent the word of authority resides in the sum total of current institutions. By this sum total I mean all ways of cooperating that at any time are commonly understood and commonly accepted. Example defines roles and points to tasks. Custom fixes requisite qualifications and links consequents to antecedents. So in the home and in the educational hierarchy, in the learned professions, in industry and commerce, in politics and finance, in church and state there develop a vast and intricate web of interconnections that set the lines along which cooperation occurs and uncooperativeness is sanctioned.

I have employed the word, institutions, in its broadest sense. It is the product of use and wont. It is the sum of the ways of cooperating that commonly are understood and commonly are accepted. It changes slowly, for a new common understanding and a new common consent are not easily developed. None the less, it is within the matrix of use and wont that power comes to be entrusted to individuals within community. There is the spontaneous articulation of the kinship group. There is the need of leaders in times of stress. There is the advantage of arbitrators in disputes. There is the role of judges in settling whether injustice has been done and, if so, what satisfaction is to be made. By way of safeguard rules of due process are devised both with regard to the selection of officials and with regard to the manner in which their office is to be fulfilled. Such rules may remain unwritten. The officials may act only in the name of some subgroup in the community. But eventually there are rules that are enacted as laws, and there are officials that act in the name of the whole community.

So we come to a distinction between authority and authorities. The authorities are the officials to whom certain offices have been entrusted and certain powers delegated. But authority belongs to the community that has a common field of experience, common and complementary ways of understanding, common judgements and common aims. It is the community that is the carrier of a common world mediated by meaning and motivated by values. It is the validity of those meanings and values that gives authority its aura and prestige.

A rhetorical and juridical concept of culture assumed that one and only one set of meanings and values was valid for all mankind. Travel and research have dissipated that illusion. There are many differentiations of human consciousness: linguistic, religious, literary, systematic, scientific, scholarly, introspective. With each differentiation there is a shift of horizon, a transformation of available meanings, a transvaluation of values. So it is that from an empirical point of view culture has come to be conceived as the set of meanings and values that inform a common way of life.

Such meanings and values may be authentic or unauthentic. They are authentic in the measure that cumulatively they are the result of the transcendental precepts, Be attentative, Be intelligent, Be reasonable, Be responsible. They are unauthentic in the measure that they are the product of cumulative inattention, obtuseness, unreasonableness, irresponsibility.

Authenticity makes power legitimate. It confers on power the aura and prestige of authority. Unauthenticity leaves power naked. It reveals power as mere power. Similarly, authenticity legitimates authorities, and unauthenticity destroys their authority and reveals them as merely powerful. Legitimated by authenticity authority and authorities have a hold on the consciences of those subject to authority and authorities. But when they lack the legitimating by authenticity, authority and authorities invite the consciences of subjects to repudiate their claims to rule. However, subjects may be authentic or unauthentic. In so far as they are authentic, they will accept the claims of legitimate authority and legitimate authorities, and they will resist the claims of illegitimate authority and illegitimate authorities. On the other hand, in so far as they are unauthentic, they will resist legitimate claims, and they will support illegitimate claims.

Dialectic has to do with the concrete, the dynamic, and the contradictory. Cooperation, power, and authority have to do with the concrete and the dynamic. Authenticity and unauthenticity add a pair of contradictories. The resulting dialectic is extremely complicated. Authenticity and unauthenticity are found in three different carriers: (1) in the community, (2) in the individuals that are authorities, and (3) in the individuals that are subject to authority. Again, unauthenticity is realized by any single act of inattention, obtuseness, unreasonableness, irresponsibility. But authenticity is reached only by long and sustained fidelity to the transcendental precepts. It exists only as a cumulatative product. Moreover, authenticity in man or woman is ever precarious: our attentiveness is ever apt to be a withdrawal from inattention; our acts of understanding a correction of our oversights; our reasonableness a victory over silliness; our responsibility a repentance for our sins. To be ever attentive, intelligent, reasonable, responsible is to live totally in the world mediated by meaning and motivated by values. But man also lives in a world of immediacy and, while the world of immediacy can be incorporated in the world mediated by meaning and motivated by values, still that incorporation never is secure. Finally, what is authentic for a lesser differentiation of consciousness will be found unauthentic by the standards of a greater differentiation. So there is a sin of backwardness, of the cultures, the authorities, the individuals that fail to live on the level of their times.

The complexity of the dialectic of authority underscores what experience has long made quite plain. Inquiry into the legitimacy of authority or authorities is complex, lengthy, tedious, and often inconclusive.

A more effective approach is to adopt a more synthetic viewpoint. The fruit of authenticity is progress. For authenticity results from a long sustained exercise of attentiveness, intelligence, reasonableness, responsibility. But long sustained attentiveness notes just what is going on. Intelligence repeatedly grasps how things can be better. Reasonableness is open to change. Responsibility weighs in the balance short and long term advantages and disadvantages, benefits and defects

The longer these four are exercised, the more certain and the greater will be the progress made.

The fruit of unauthenticity is decline. Unauthentic subjects get themselves unauthentic authorities. Unauthentic authorities favor some groups over others. Favoritism breeds suspicion, distrust, dissension, opposition, hatred, violence. Community loses its common aims and begins to operate at cross-purposes. It loses its common judgements so that different groups inhabit different worlds. Common understanding is replaced by mutual incomprehension. The common field of experience is divided into hostile territories.

The breakdown of community entails the breakdown of cooperation. Different groups advocate different policies. Different policies entail different plans, and the different groups deploy all their resources for the implementation of the plans that accord with their policies. There may be a seesaw battle between them with the resultant incoherence and confusion. Or one side may gain the upperhand and then exploitation of the other follows.

Just as sustained authenticity results in increasing responsibility and order, increasing reasonableness and cohesion, increasing intelligence and objective intelligibility, increasing knowledge and mastery of the situation, so sustained unauthenticity has the opposite effects. But the remedy for the opposite effects lies beyond any normal human procedure. There is no use appealing to the sense of responsibility of irresponsible people, to the reasonableness of people that are unreasonable, to the intelligence of people that have chosen to be obtuse, to the attention of people that attend only to their grievances. Again, the objective situation brought about by sustained unauthenticity is not an intelligible situation. It is the product of inattention, obtuseness, unreasonableness, irresponsibility. It is an objective surd, the realization of the irrational. A natural situation yields fruits a hundredfold to the sustained application of intelligence. But an irrational situation is just stony ground, and to apply intelligence to it yields nothing.

However, beyond progress and decline there is redemption. Its principle is self-sacrificing love. To fall in love is to go beyond attention, intelligence, reasonableness, responsibility. It is to set up a new principle that has, indeed, its causes, conditions, and occassions but, as long as it lasts, provides the mainsprnig of one's desire and fear, hope and despair, joy and sorrow. In the measure that the community becomes a community of love and so capable of making real and great sacrifices, in that measure it can wipe out the grievances and correct the objective absurdities that its unauthenticity has brought about.

I speak of redemption from within the Christian tradition, in which Christ suffering, dying, and rising again is at once the motive and the model of self-sacrificing love. But if one is willing to attend to the ideal types propounded by Arnold Toynbee in his *Study of History*, a more general statement is possible. In that study of course Toynbee thought he was contributing to empirical science. Since then however he has recanted. But, I believe, his work remains a contribution not to knowledge of reality, not to hypotheses about reality, but to the ideal types that are intelligible sets of concepts and often prove useful to have at hand when it comes to describing reality or to forming hypotheses about it.

Relevant to present purposes would be Toynbee's creative minority, his dominant minority, his internal and external proletariat, and his universal religion within which a new civilisation arises from the disorder and conflicts of the old. The creative minority are the representatives of progress. They are the leaders that gain the adhesion of the masses by successfully meeting the challenge of each successive situation. The dominant minority are the representatives of decline. They inherit the power of the creative minority, but they are unable to solve the problems that continuously multiply. The internal proletariat is constituted by the increasingly disaffected and disillusioned masses. The external proletariat are the less developed foreign peoples that are beginning to discover the weaknesses of their envied neighbor. In modern dress the internal and external proletariats would have to be related to John Kenneth Galbraith's multinational corporations. Religion, finally, in an era of crisis has to think less of issuing commands and decrees and more of fostering the self-sacrificing love that alone is capable of providing the solution to the evils of decline and of reinstating the beneficent progress that is entailed by sustained authenticity.

I have placed the legitimacy of authority in its authenticity. But besides the legitimacy of authority, there also is the assertion of that legitimacy, its legitimation. Legitimation is manifold. It occurs on any of the many differentiations of consciousness. In early human society it is a matter of myth and ritual. In the ancient high civilizations it became a matter of law. Among the loquacious and literary Greeks law was reinforced first by rhetoric and later by logic. Historians discovered that different laws obtained at different times and places. Systematizers sought to draw up codes that would express the eternal verities for all times and places. Philosophers sought principles that would underpin this or that system. But if the legitimacy of authority lies in its authenticity, none of these solutions is adequate.

By this I do not mean to deny what already I have affirmed. Besides authority there also are needed authorities. If there are to be authorities, then over and above their authenticity there is needed some external criterion by which their position can be publicly recognized. But while this external criterion is a necessary condition, it is not a sufficient condition. The sufficient condition must include authenticity. The external criterion need not be accompanied by authenticity. For in human beings authenticity always is precarious. Commonly, indeed, it is no more than a withdrawal from unauthenticity.

Such then is the dialectic of authority. It was well expressed by Barbara Barclay Carter in her preface to her translation of Don Luigi Sturzo's *Church and State* when she wrote: "... in every form of social life and in human society as a whole two currents are invariably present, the *'organisational'* and the *'mystical'* or ideal, the one tending to conservation, to practical constructions that perpetuate an established order, the other to renewal, with sharpened awareness of present deficiencies and impellent awareness towards a better future. The distinction between them is never absolute, for they are made up of human individuals and reflect the complexity of human minds; their action is an interweaving, the one eventually consolidating something of what the other conceives, yet they come together only to part anew; the conflict they manifest is the conflict between the ideal and its always only partial realisation, between the letter that kills and the spirit that quickens, and while the Church is essentially the expression of the mystical current in the face of the State ... in the Church as in the State the two forces are perennially working."[1]

---

[1] Luigi Sturzo, *Church and State*, London: Geoffrey Bles, 1939, p. 6.

AUTHORITY AND MORALITY*

RICHARD T. DE GEORGE

Authority has been widely attacked in recent years, most frequently in the name of morality and freedom. But a systematic account of the relation of authority and morality has yet to be made. It is the aim of this paper to help provide such an account. In the course of my analysis I shall attempt to clarify some of the ways in which and the extent to which morality and authority are compatible.

I

The relation of authority and morality is frequently oversimplified because of a simplistic view of the nature of authority which identifies it with executive authority or with the right or power to command or to force another to act in a certain way. Starting from this view of authority there are two arguments which have been frequently used to show the incompatibility of authority and morality. The first is based on the source of morality and of moral norms and values; the second, on an analysis of moral autonomy or freedom. Each makes a valid point. But instead of their conclusions being the end of an investigation of authority and morality, they provide simply a beginning.

(1) The first argument goes roughly as follows, and depends on what it means for there to be a moral authority. A moral authority is someone who has the right and the power to dictate what men ought to do insofar as their actions are right or wrong, and to reward or punish them according to whether or not they act as he commands. Someone is a moral authority, on this view, if he is the author of morality, and if it is his decision or command which makes actions right or wrong. The paradigm of such a moral legislator and executive is God, though in certain

---

* This paper was written while I was being partially supported by a Project Grant from the National Endowment for the Humanities. The findings and views presented in this paper, however, do not necessarily represent the view of the Endowment.

eras and in certain social systems he might be the king or ruler or Party. But what can it mean for the rightness or wrongness of an action to be determined by such an authority? Either (a) his decision about the moral quality of an action is arbitrary and dependent only on his whim; or (b) he has some criteria by which to decide which actions are good and which are not.

(a) Consider the first alternative. Suppose that an action is right or wrong only because someone in authority says it is so. Then what it means for an action to be right or wrong is for it to be judged so by the authority.

It is clear that this is not what most men mean by "good" or "bad," "right" or "wrong." But even if someone (or some group) were to mean this by these terms, would he continue to do so if he analyzed what this entails? It would seem that if he were a reasonable person, he could not. For he would have to have some good reason for accepting the fiat of the one in authority; and no such good reason is available. The most plausible reasons, and the ones usually given for such acceptance are either that (i) the moral lawgiver is powerful and will punish those who do not follow his commands; or that (ii) he is himself good, can command only what is good, and so should be obeyed.

(i) The first reason is fear of punishment, here or hereafter. But clearly such fear is not an adequate basis for obeying an authority's commands. If someone who is powerful were to command an act which is immoral, the subject of that command might well perform it out of fear. But his performance of an immoral action, though itself an instance of obedience, would not change the nature of the act performed. On the view being considered, however, an action commanded by the moral authority could not be immoral, because what it means for an action to be wrong is for it to be held wrong by the one in authority. The result of this view is that any action – no matter how vile by any reasonable standard – would be moral as long as commanded, arbitrarily or not, by the one in authority. The murder of millions, the wanton infliction of pain, the senseless maiming of the innocent – all of these would become moral actions which must be performed when commanded by the authority if one wished to act morally. Any enlightened person could scarcely take this view as a serious account either of what most men mean or of what they should mean when they speak of morality. The power to force a subject to act in the way one demands is insufficient, therefore, to make an action moral, if "moral" is to be understood in any ordinary sense.

(ii) The other alternative was that an action was held to be good because it was commanded by one in authority, and he would not command what is evil because he himself is good. Thus, it is maintained, God's commands are good, what He commands is moral, because He Himself is all good and incapable of commanding what is evil.

In examining this claim we once again have two choices. For either (α) what God commands is good because it emanates from Him, and He is good; or (β) God is good because He always commands what is in fact good independent of His command; which implies that He has some criteria for deciding what is good and what is bad.

(α) Consider the first alternative. What could the claim that God (or some similar moral authority) is good mean to the man who is searching for the basis of morality? If whatever God commands is good, and if we are not to fall back into the previous case in which even the most heinous crimes become good because commanded by God or some other authority, then there must be some other sense given to the statement that the authority is good. The ordinary means of judging whether someone is good is by examining his actions. But this is precisely what in this case we are precluded from doing. For on this view what the authority commands is good simply because it is commanded. There is thus no independent way to judge the goodness or badness of the commands because what is being denied is any criterion outside of the authority's commands. As a result there is no way to judge that the authority is good. Yet the argument depends on the judgment that he is good. It thus assumes precisely that goodness which it is its aim to explain.

One might attempt to save the argument in two ways. The first would be to maintain that on some independent grounds one can judge that the authority is good, and once this judgment has been made then it can be held with confidence that anything he commands, even if we do not see why it is good, is good. This is an application of the type of argument I shall examine more carefully later. But the present point is that this argument presupposes the validity of some judgments based on criteria other than the goodness of the Lawgiver or moral executive. If this is the case, however, then first there are independent means of determining what is right and wrong, good and bad, which are logically prior to the criterion of the authority's fiat; and second, the meaning of the terms is not dependent on the lawgiver. If the independent judgments are valid for deciding that the authority is in fact good, why can they not be used to constantly check on him to decide in each continuing case that he is good? There may be instances in which it is reasonable to hold that his judgment on a given moral issue is correct even though one does not see the reasons clearly one self. But this is not the same as saying that what is commanded is right simply because it is commanded by the authority. The possibility of independent judgment must be available; and in fact it must be assumed that the authority is judging on the basis of greater insight into the criteria available. Hence this version of the argument fails to substantiate the view that what is right or good is made right or good simply by the arbitrary decision of an authority.

A second way one might attempt to save the argument is to claim simply that he holds on faith that the lawgiver is good, and accepts whatever he says in this regard. There is no arguing with someone who baldly makes this assertion and feels no need for any rational defense of his position. If his leap of faith is indeed not to be rationally defended, and no claim is made for its rationality, then argument or reasons are to no avail. This move takes morality outside of the realm of rational consideration, and someone defending this view cannot at the same time maintain it and consistently claim to be holding a rationally justifiable position. His morality thus is removed from the realm of rational consideration, and as far as reason is concerned it becomes arbitrary, and indistinguishable from the arbitrary decisions of the lawgiver. It thus collapses into the first type of case which we examined. An alternative version of this argument consists in asserting that the lawgiver, if he is in fact also the Maker of the beings He commands, has the right to command His subjects as He wills. This, too, however, either collapses into case (i) or into a view which the term "right" and the criteria for moral goodness are in some sense independent of the lawmaker's whim.

There is a further difficulty with either variation of this type of view of a moral authority. Suppose that one holds that what is right or wrong is determined by the fiat of a moral authority, and that somehow a consistent interpretation can be given to this. How could moral agents ever know what actions to perform? How could they know which actions were right and which ones wrong? If all actions are right or wrong only by the decision of an authority, then we would all have to wait after each act for him to pass his judgment. It would be insufficient for him to simply make known to us by some means a general set of rules; for at any time he might change the rules and make what was right wrong and what was bad good. Hence on such a view we could never know which acts were right and which wrong. Since, furthermore, no rule can cover all situations, rules would need interpreting in different situations. But unless somehow we were told in each specific instance what the correct interpretation was, we would not know how to act in order to behave morally. It is clear that no human authority could possibly give us each his interpretation, even if like Big Brother in *1984* he constantly surveyed each of our actions with his electronic equipment. But if the moral authority is God, then in fact He can, it is claimed, keep track of all our actions and dictate what we should do. To consistently maintain this view, however, it is necessary that He do more than issue the Ten Commandments and perhaps establish a Church or some authorized body of interpreters to whom He communicates His views. For what is needed is a direct line with all moral men. On either view, whether we consider a special group to be the interpreters of His desires or whether each man has a direct line to the moral authority through something like conscience, what must be made clear is how the authority's decisions in each case are communicated. Some may claim that they simply know directly how the moral authority evaluates a situation, calling it inspiration or moral intuition. How such knowledge can be verified, however, if – as is frequently the case – equally sincere and believing people disagree on the moral quality of a particular action, remains an unanswerable question if no criterion is to be allowed other than the authority's fiat.

(β) If we argue that God is good because He always commands what is in fact good independent of His command, we are forced to acknowledge some criterion for His deciding what is good and what is bad. What is really being denied on this view is the arbitrariness of God's commands. The attempt is both to say that God is not arbitrary and yet to maintain that morality at least in some sense comes from Him. One standard way to argue this is to claim that God is rational, and so He made things and the rules by which they are governed not arbitrarily but for good reasons. Another is to maintain that He made the world and men according to certain laws of His choosing. These laws of nature can be discovered by men; but they are dependent on God in the first place, and He could have made them differently. On any version, however, whether one appeals to the nature of reason or to the natural law, he acknowledges a criterion independent of an authority's command, even if he maintains that metaphysically the criterion is dependent on the authority.

The overall conclusion, the argument goes, is that the only reasonable position to adopt is alternative (β), which holds that the moral authority designates certain actions good because by some criterion or criteria he knows they are good. It is because they are good that he says they are; it is not the case that they are good because he says so. But if actions are good independently of his saying so, if they are moral independent of his command, then the source of their goodness must be something other than his fiat or command. Furthermore, the criterion or criteria must be available to others. Otherwise they could never judge that the moral authority and his actions and decisions were good, and so they would not know that they should accept what he says. But if what is good and what is bad are not dependent on his fiat, then we should attempt to uncover the grounds for the goodness and badness of actions. The difficulty of discovering what the authority says, of interpreting it, and of deciding whether it is in fact moral is greater and involves more chance of error than discovering simply whether the action is moral or immoral. Since this can be discovered independently of the moral lawgiver, the moral lawgiver becomes superfluous for this purpose. God or the Church or the State or some other authority may know better than the ordinary man what is right or wrong; but this is beside the point. For neither the meaning of "good" and "bad" nor the morality of any action is dependent on the command of the lawgiver or of the moral authority. As a consequence, the moral man stands in no need of an executive moral authority. Morality is autonomous and not authority-dependent.

(2) The second argument generally brought against authority in morality is based on a view of the autonomy of the moral agent. It can be summarized as follows. What it means for someone to be a moral agent is for him to freely choose an action and accept responsibility for it. Though he may seek advice from others, ultimately he must decide for himself how he is to act and take responsibility for his action. Only in so doing is he a full moral agent.

In the Kantian version of this argument the moral agent's autonomy involves being his own lawgiver. But this does not mean that he can make up any moral laws he wishes. He must follow the dictates of reason and the universal laws which it prescribes. He is to act on the moral law because it is his duty to so act. Only then is he, strictly speaking, moral. Thus, to act simply on the command of another, to give over one's responsibility, to give up one's moral autonomy, is to cease to be a fully moral agent. On the Sartrian view to give up one's moral autonomy in this way would be to act in bad faith, i.e., to act as if one were not free.

In any version of this argument a moral action is not simply one that coincides with what is morally obligatory. If an action is to have subjective moral worth it must be performed by one who freely chooses to do it, which precludes his doing it simply because it is commanded. For to act on the command of a moral authority is to withhold one's judgment as to the moral worth of an action or to assume its morality simply because it is commanded. In this case it is obvious that one is not legislating for oneself, that he is giving up his autonomy, and to that extent is no longer a full moral agent. Children may have the obligation to obey their parents; but this is a reflection of the fact that they are not fully developed rational beings. Mature adults, if they are to exercise their full moral capacities, cannot simply do what another says merely because he commands it. This would make obedience to authority the only moral commandment. Every act would be only an act of obedience, without consideration of the nature of the action commanded. The agent would thereby relinquish responsibility for the morality of the action commanded, and to that extent he would fail to act morally. Hence, the argument goes, moral autonomy of the individual is incompatible with moral authority.

II.

Both of the preceding arguments have a valid point. First, morality is autonomous, in the sense that it is not simply the arbitrary fiat of someone in authority; actions are right or wrong, good or bad, because of something other than an authority's say so. Second, all rational men can in principle arrive at a determination of moral rules or values or particular obligations. The individual rational being is morally autonomous in the sense that ultimately he must make his own choice as to how to act and accept the responsibility for such actions. But admitting all of this, it would be a mistake to conclude that there is no legitimate moral authority or that authority and morality are antithetical. For to do so would be to fail to consider carefully enough either the nature of authority or the actual moral situation in which men find themselves acting as moral agents.

One of the limitations of our discussion of authority thus far has been that we have been talking only about a moral legislator, someone in authority who gives commands which must be obeyed simply because he has given them. Executive authority, or the right to command, is certainly one type of authority, and the type taken as the paradigm in the political realm. But it is not the only kind of authority, and it is in fact the wrong paradigm to take if one wants to consider the true function of authority in morality.

We can distinguish four types of authority in morality. We have already seen the type of authority characteristic of the moral lawgiver, or executive moral authority. The second type is the authority which a person frequently has who is especially knowledgeable in a field of learning. We speak of an authority in Greek history, or of an authority in constitutional law. Similarly, if morality involves knowledge of right and wrong, as many claim it does, then we can speak of epistemic moral authority. Thirdly, men often find their moral values exemplified in a particularly dramatic, moving, and inspiring way by some holy man or saint or moral hero. The authority of such a person can be called exemplary moral authority. The fourth type is the authority which characterizes the actions of a person who acts as morality obliges. He has the moral authority to do certain actions or refrain from doing others. I shall speak of such cases as a person's having the authority of moral obligation. Though related, each of the four types can and should, for clarity's sake, be distinguished. In the remainder of this paper I shall attempt to clarify each of these types of authority and examine their legitimacy and their function.

The epistemic moral authority is similar to any other type of epistemic authority, and subject to similar restraints on his legitimacy. An epistemic moral authority is someone who has knowledge in the moral realm. It may be knowledge of moral principles; expertise in moral reasoning or in the application of such principles to specific cases; or knowledge of conventional norms, i.e., of what is generally held to be right and wrong by a community or society. Someone is a moral authority for another, that is, he is a *de facto* epistemic moral authority, if what he says in the moral realm is believed by the other person, and held by the latter to be true or more probably true than before the authority was consulted, simply because the authority has spoken. The authority in this case might be an individual person, or a group (such as a Church), or a book such as the Bible or an ethics text. In each case the subject of authority believes what the authority says and so constitutes him as a *de facto* authority. But such an authority may be either a legitimate authority or not, depending on whether in fact he has the knowledge he is presumed to have and whether or not what he says is in fact the case. Someone could be a *de facto* epistemic moral authority even if there were no such thing as moral knowledge. He could not, however, be a legitimate authority, as I am using the term. Similarly someone might have true knowledge of what is right and what is wrong, and so have what is necessary for his being a legitimate authority, without ever being recognized by anyone as an authority and so without ever being a *de facto* authority. The extent of one's authority is a function of the number of persons for whom he is an authority; the intensity of his authority is a function of the degree of acceptance actually given his assertions by those who accept his authority.

If parents are *de facto* epistemic moral authorities for their children, this means that what they say in the moral realm is believed to a greater or lesser degree by their children. Children do well to learn from their parents, as well as from their teachers and other adults, in the moral as in other realms, because children know so little in comparison with adults that they cannot help but learn a great deal that is correct by believing what they are told, even if in the process they learn something that is false. As they grow, children become more discriminating in what they believe in the moral as in other realms. Where there is disagreement among authorities, they rightly attach less credence to the statements of any of the authorities than when there is agreement among them. This in part accounts for the difficulty in transmitting moral norms and values in a dynamic, pluralistic society as opposed to a traditional, monolithic one.

Epistemic moral authority is by its very nature substitutional, as is all epistemic authority. It is in principle possible for others to achieve the knowledge that the moral authority has, and as the subject of authority acquires more of that knowledge he needs the authority less. In the moral realm it should be the aim of a moral teacher to enable the subjects of his authority eventually to make their own moral decisions, for it is only when they reach this level that they become fully moral and responsible. This is one of the ways in which moral epistemic authority is substitutional. Parents tell their children what is right and wrong and counsel them until they are able to make the necessary discriminations, carry on the moral reasoning process, and make moral evaluations on their own.

But there is a second sense in which moral epistemic authority is substitutional. It is possible for adults also to need help with their moral reasoning, to seek advice and moral guidance, and so it is possible and frequently the case that they seek out an epistemic moral authority. Since they are not subject to anyone in the sense that a child is subject to his parents and dependent on them, their choice of a moral authority is one which they themselves make. Epistemic moral authorities may be formally designated in a society or they may be informally identified by an individual on his own. In each case the logic behind the identification is similar.

The subject of moral authority must have at least some knowledge of the field if he is to make the identification himself. He must know something about what is moral and what not, he must know what moral knowledge is like, and he must believe that he has some such knowledge himself. Otherwise he will not be able to recognize someone who has it. He must, that is, be able to verify by some independent means at least some of the moral statements of the person he will accept as an authority. He must also be able to follow at least to some extent the reasoning by which the authority arrives at his conclusions. To be able to do that much serves as a basis upon which to feel – rightly or wrongly – that when the authority goes beyond him, when he is unable to follow his reasoning or principles, he nonetheless has good reason for accepting his conclusions. He will in this way have some grounds for believing the authority to be a legitimate authority, and for his making him a *de facto* authority. The amount of credence he gives the authority may vary from very slight belief in what he says to complete belief, weighed against whatever else pertinent the subject knows, the other opinions or statements or beliefs pertinent to the moral situation he has encountered, the satisfactoriness of the advice he has received in the past, and so on. It takes many correct utterances in an area to build up a basis for confidence in an authority. It takes very few discovered errors to undermine such confidence.

The situation is similar for a formally designated moral authority. An informal moral authority for an individual might be his friend or loved one whom he feels knows more or is more morally sensitive than he himself. A formally recognized authority is one whom society or some portion of it designates as having more than usual competence in an area because of study or training of a certain type. Thus moral philosophers or ordained ministers are certified as having spent a certain number of years studying moral theory or casuistry or other pertinent materials. Society's stamp signifies that some process similar to that described above with respect to an individual has been gone through for a class of persons. Just as doctors or lawyers are certified, so are ministers or moral philosophers. Such certification designates an individual as a member of a class. That he in fact has more knowledge in the moral realm, and that he is able to communicate it, is something to which most persons who have not studied the field to the same extent might be willing to give *prima facie* credence; though the subject would do well to test the knowledge of the authority he chooses just as he tests the knowledge of someone not formally certified. The acceptance of the pronouncements of a clergyman by his flock is a paradigm of the case of an officially certified moral authority who becomes for many a *de facto* moral authority.

Disagreements among authorities, however, tend to undermine the authority of all of them. This is clearly seen to be the case when within a given church or society formal epistemic moral authorities differ as to the morality of birth control or abortion or divorce; and it is also the case when differing sects or segments of the society hold varying views on the morality of an act or on moral values.

Epistemic moral authority is based on the real or purported moral knowledge of the authority relative to the moral knowledge of the subject. But since morality is a realm of practical activity one can be an authority not only because of his knowledge but also because of his virtue. In this latter case he would be an exemplary moral authority. An epistemic moral authority is supposed to have knowledge in the moral realm; it is not necessary for him to act in accordance with that knowledge, that is, it is not necessary for him to act virtuously, though one may well question the depth of his knowledge or the sincerity of his belief if he consistently acted in opposition to his stated beliefs on moral issues. It is not necessary, however, that such an authority be especially moral for him to be good at moral reasoning. Weakness of will and knowledge of moral principles are compatible.

An exemplary moral authority is one whose actions inspire others or one whose actions become a model for the behavior of others. Once again an exemplary moral authority may be a *de facto* authority, a legitimate authority, or both. Also, as in the case of an epistemic moral authority, in order for an exemplary moral authority to become a *de facto* authority the subject of his authority must have enough insight into the moral nature of his activities to recognize his actions as good or right or as embodying moral values. Saints and the recounted lives of saints, holy men, and moral personalities or heroes all serve as exemplary moral authorities for many who look to their actions as an inspiration or as a guide to how they should behave. As in the case of epistemic moral authority, someone may see in the actions of a friend, associate, neighbor, or loved one exemplary moral conduct; and so he may choose not only to act as that person does, follow in the causes he champions, live in his style, but also he may seek him out for moral advice. In the latter case he might hold what the other says to be the case not because of any reasons or principles that the latter is able to articulate, but because he trusts the intuitive judgment of the authority, based on his acceptance of his judgments and of his actions in previous circumstances.

Moral values and attitudes are often communicated more effectively by example than by preaching; moral reasoning, by teaching and explanation rather than simply by acting. Clearly, however, epistemic moral authority and exemplary moral authority, though distinguishable, are very closely related and are frequently found together. The great moral teachers have most often been moral exemplars as well.

Thus far I have been maintaining that it is reasonable and legitimate to accept authority in morality under certain circumstances; that children do learn from their parents, their elders, and their peers, as well as from their own experience; and that adults similarly can legitimately seek advice and consult others about their moral difficulties and dilemmas. But this implies neither that a moral authority can absolve a moral agent of his responsibility to make his own moral decisions and to accept the responsibility for those decisions, nor that a moral authority has the right to command the actions of any individual. Neither epistemic nor exemplary moral authority entails executive moral authority, and they should be clearly distinguished from it.

Someone is a *de facto* executive moral authority if either his commands constitute for another what is moral or immoral or if he enforces his moral code by acting on or for another and such action is accepted by that other as legitimate. The right to executive moral authority has at various times been claimed to be a function of knowledge, of virtue, or of position. Is such authority ever legitimate? From the above analysis of epistemic and exemplary moral authority it should be clear that neither of them (nor the two together) entails any right to command; hence executive moral authority cannot be justified or rendered legitimate in terms of one's moral knowledge or virtue alone.

An epistemic or exemplary moral authority may give commands, tell others what to do, or act on or for them; and his actions may be accepted and his commands obeyed. He thus may be a *de facto* executive moral authority. The reason he cannot be a legitimate executive moral authority on the basis of his knowledge alone is that knowledge in the realm of morals, as in any other realm, is insufficient by itself to bestow any right to command. Hence if someone either believes or knows that a certain action is right or wrong, this knowledge by itself does not bestow any *right* on him to force an action on another. He himself may have an obligation to act in a certain way, or to try to inform others of the proper way to act. But his knowledge, real or purported, *by itself* is not sufficient to give him the right to act.

This assertion must be correctly understood. Knowledge of one's obligation entails the moral duty to fulfill that obligation. But knowledge of someone else's obligation, or knowledge that some action which is going to be performed by someone else is wrong, does not give anyone the right to command that person or to interfere with his action or force him to act otherwise. If some harm is to befall another, then one may have the obligation to protect that other. But this is different from having the right to command another or to force him to act in a certain way *simply* because of one's moral knowledge or virtue. If, for instance, someone knew that serving in the army, or practicing segregation, or engaging in prostitution were wrong, he would not, simply in virtue of this knowledge, have the right to forcibly prevent those wishing to do any of these things. He might speak against such actions, attempt to get legislation to outlaw them, or take other steps in virtue of his rights as a citizen, but not in virtue of his knowledge alone. The preacher or the prophet may have the duty to extol others to act in certain ways; but neither his virtue nor his knowledge gives him any special right to act on or for others. His words and actions may draw followers who do as he says simply because he says so. They may so act because they accept that what he says is in fact right for some valid reason other than his saying so; in which case they are not so much doing what he says simply in response to his *command* as acting in response to the moral imperative which he clarifies or enunciates for them. They may, on the other hand, act simply because he commands them. The second instance, as we have already seen, is not legitimate; the first is legitimate, but as described it is not an instance of executive moral authority.

An epistemic moral authority may be approached by someone for moral guidance. If the inquirer receives such guidance, he may be immoral if he does not act on it. But the one from whom he received the guidance has no right to force him to act as morality demands. He can legitimately only inform him of the moral nature of the act and of the reasons which substantiate his evaluation. Similarly the saint or holy man inspires by his actions. He may exhort others as well to act as he does. But he has no right to force them to so act. This follows from the nature of morality and from the autonomy of the moral agent. A moral agent can rightly seek advice and should act on the best advice and insight he can muster. But the action remains his, and he retains responsibility for it.

If we see the legitimate function of a moral authority as one who teaches what is right or who exemplifies what is good, then the model of a moral authority is not that of an executive giving orders but of a teacher showing the way. The better he does his job, the less he is needed.

An individual's conscience is the proximate and in that sense the ultimate authority for him in moral matters. This simply means that in the end the moral agent must decide for himself how he is to act. The moral teacher can say what he believes to be right and wrong; and a good teacher of those who have reached moral maturity will also explain why and how that judgment was arrived at, what rules or principles were pertinent, and what values were involved. His reasoning can thus be followed and checked.

No one's conscience is incorrigible or infallible. It may be mistaken. But the moral man is obliged to act according to the dictates of his conscience, where this means that he is obliged to act on the basis of the best moral deliberation he is capable of at the time, taking into account all the pertinent facts, values, principles, and circumstances. He may be mistaken in perceiving his duty, and he has the obligation to try to perceive his duty to the best of his ability. But ultimately his action has subjective moral value only if he acts as his conscience says he should. In this sense one's conscience is a moral authority issuing commands; the commands, however, are to oneself and are binding on oneself and not on anyone else. The authority of one's conscience as thus explained is compatible both with learning from an epistemic or exemplary moral authority and with denying the right to command as a function of knowledge or virtue.

Legitimate executive moral authority, the right to command and legitimately expect obedience, is found in the case of parents with respect to their young children and in the case of others who stand in a similar relation to those who are not fully capable of taking on moral responsibility. Executive moral authority is here a function both of the position of the bearers of authority and the incomplete moral development of the subjects of such authority. With children the period is one of training and forming habits of virtue; obedience is the initial virtue through which the habits are formed. But as their children develop, parents should help them become fully autonomous moral persons; obedience becomes less and less necessary and less and less the exclusive virtue.

In an age or in a society in which all men are expected to act like children in the realm of morality, obedience may be the only virtue. But for a society of mature moral individuals any church or body which is a moral authority is such in virtue of its acceptance by its adherents who learn from it or who find in it examples of virtue. This is one of the elements which separate members of a church, for instance, from non-members. The former find examples of wisdom and virtue in the church despite obvious defects, while non-members frequently focus on the defects and are not touched by the examples of virtue or are not persuaded by the moral reasoning of its leaders.

In a society of fully moral agents is there any legitimate executive moral authority? We have seen that neither knowledge nor virtue confers such legitimacy, and that position does so only with respect to parents and their children. To claim that there is no other legitimate executive *moral* authority is not to claim that there is no legitimate executive authority, nor to claim that such authority is never morally grounded.

A government may, for instance, pass laws in virtue of its imperial authority, i.e., in virtue of some system of laws by which it is empowered to do so. Ideally it should act with knowledge; but clearly its authority to pass laws does not stem only from its knowledge. Its executive authority has its basis in the state's constitution or in tradition or in an original contract or in something else of the kind. Its executive authority has a moral basis if its issuing of laws or commands is morally justifiable and if the laws or commands it issues are not themselves immoral. But a citizen's *prima facie legal* obligation to obey laws of the land never overrides his *moral* obligation to act in accordance with his conscience. Hence the executive authority of a government is not executive *moral* authority.

The phrase "executive moral authority" is thus somewhat ambiguous. I have been arguing that except with respect to parents and their children (and similar cases) it is never legitimate for anyone to command another in such a way that the command constitutes what is right or wrong for the other, nor is it legitimate to force another to act in certains ways *simply* because of one's moral knowledge. I have *not* been arguing that no one has the right to command others or that such (non-moral) executive authority cannot be morally justified.

Throughout our discussion thus far there has been hovering in the background the presupposition that there is such a thing as morality which involves moral principles, values, and ideals. It is in fact because we seek to learn more about these that we turn to epistemic moral authorities; and it is because they embody such values and ideals in their actions and act so clearly on such principles that exemplary moral authorities exert such an influence. Ultimately it is the principles, values, and ideals which are at the basis of all moral authority, just as it is the ground of truth which is at the basis of all epistemic authority.

The fourth type of moral authority is thus basic to the others. The authority of moral obligation is the right to act as I am morally obliged to act. Since I have the obligation to act as duty commands, I have the right to so act; and to act in this way is to act in a manner authorized by morality, or to act with moral authority. Any moral action can thus be spoken of as carrying moral authority, or the person performing the action may be said to be acting with moral authority. His actions are authorized by the demands of morality.

The phrase "moral authority" is sometimes used to characterize the actions of those who act with confidence and assurance that their actions are morally correct, and so it is used to describe the psychological state of the agent rather than the action itself. Someone who is convinced of the morality of his action, whether or not his action is actually objectively moral and whether or not he has the right to force it upon others, may in an authoritative manner perform some given action or attempt to enforce his view. He may act as if he had the moral authority to so act whether he has such authority or not. His assurance and the strength of his belief may be sufficient to render him a *de facto* epistemic or exemplary moral authority and for others to consider his actions to have *de facto* moral authority and to accept them. But legitimate moral authority accrues to moral actions and only to moral actions, irrespective of the psychological confidence or lack of confidence of the agent.

If everyone should act as he is morally obliged to act, and if ultimately he must be the judge of this moral obligation, then everyone must act as he thinks he is morally obliged to act. The discrepancy between what morality demands and what someone thinks morality demands, however, also makes it legitimate for individuals or groups or societies to defend themselves not only against the wrongdoings of others but also against what they perceive as such wrongdoings.

From a social point of view no unjust law can bind the conscience of any member of a society, each of whom must act in accordance with what he believes to be his obligation or duty. A citizen is thus not morally obliged to obey any and every law passed by any government, state, or society. He may be *legally* obliged to obey all the laws of a country, and he may – if he believes them to be wrong (whether or not they in fact are) – be simultaneously *morally* obliged to act at variance with some of them. Nonetheless a government, state, or society may attach penalties to disobedience or failure to comply with its laws, and it has the *prima facie* legal right to take appropriate action against the lawbreaker. Since no individual and no collective is infallible, where there is a conflict over whether a particular action is moral or not, both sides to the dispute should be willing rationally to consider all the facts, principles, and values at issue. The moral right to civil disobedience does not carry with it the right to inflict injury on others, unless the infliction of such injury is a moral obligation or the indirect and legitimate result of performing a morally required action. If a civil disobedient has as his aim the raising of the question of the legitimacy or morality of certain laws or governmental actions, then the authorities in a government should pay attention to his claims, though they are not required to pardon any or all such disobedients simply because they claim to be acting on the basis of their consciences.

Moral authority is the authority to act as one is morally required; but this is consistent with others so acting, and with each protecting himself and refraining from doing injury to others.

Law and government may be considered from a strictly positivistic viewpoint as a self-sufficient system based on agreements or contracts; or they may be considered to have a moral basis, legitimate governments being morally authorized to perform the tasks they do perform. It is not the aim of this paper to settle that issue. Imperial authority or civil authority may be morally based or not; and if morally based, a government or its agents may act in accordance with the demands of morality or not. From a moral point of view those subject to such executive authority clearly are never morally obliged to act in ways they perceive as immoral. Nor is the question of whether those in government should legislate morality a topic to be decided simply by studying moral authority. We have seen that knowledge or virtue by themselves do not involve the right to command. A government's legal right to command should not be confused with executive moral authority. Though no government has the right to legislate what is immoral, it is fairly clear that it is not required to legislate and enforce all that is required by morality, because it could not possibly do so. The extent to which it should go in legislating and enforcing by the means at its disposal what is morally required is a function of the type of society it is, the type of executive (non-moral) authority it has, the quality of life and the moral development of its citizens, its own moral knowledge, the amount of disruption the society can stand in allowing diversity of moral views free reign, and so on.

Morality arises in a social setting in part from the necessity of balancing individual freedom and individual protection. To act freely one must be secure in the knowledge that he will be allowed to perform certain actions without interference. Otherwise the scope of one's actions would be severely restricted by acts of self-protection. Part of the function of a society and of laws or rules within that society is to foster the freedom, through fostering the security, of the members of that society. Freedom and security are included in the values to be weighed and balanced in a moral society.

Moral authority is frequently taken as being overriding. It is properly so taken if this means that one's moral obligation, as he perceives it, is the basis on which one should act, despite opposing legal or other rules to the contrary. But only the foolish man or the fanatic ignores the possibility of his being mistaken in his perception of what morality actually requires when he encounters tradition, rules, laws, values, principles and so on which weigh against his own perceptions. These should all be considered. But in the end he should act as he believes he is morally required to act.

The conclusion we have arrived at is that, given the autonomy of morality and the moral autonomy of the individual person, epistemic and exemplary moral authority are in certain cases legitimate and compatible with them. Executive moral authority cannot be derived from either knowledge or virtue alone, and the right to command morality is restricted to parents over young children and others in similar situations. The basis for such executive moral authority as well as for epistemic and exemplary moral authority is ultimately what is commanded by morality itself. Moral authority may ground both individual and social actions. But socially, such authority by itself is insufficient ground for legislating morality, since other factors – position, the legal framework, and similar considerations – must also be taken into account. In the last analysis each person has the moral authority to act as he should, despite the problems raised by the slippage between what morality actually demands and his subjective perception of those demands.

Authority and morality are thus neither as close as some have maintained, nor as antithetical as others would have us believe. Authority is in certain circumstances compatible with morality. But as we have seen care must be taken to distinguish various types of authority and to ferret out their multiple links with morality.

STOOPING TO CONQUER:
REFLECTIONS ON AUTHORITY

WILLIAM H. DAVIS

Every man wishes to be a free spirit. Everyone longs for an unhampered, unbounded expression of his will. Perhaps nowhere is this truth so evident as in babies. I do not know whether the fetus feels frustration and rage, but the newborn infant finds its desires thwarted at every turn. The baby feels the world as an intolerable resistance against his will. But no less is this true of the adult. Moreover, adults have a powerful imagination which vastly enlarges the scope of their desires and places before the mind's eye the whole universe as a field to overcome.

On any view of man, the completely free exercise of the will is impossible. No one can indulge himself utterly. For one thing, the world is only plastic to our desires up to a point; beyond that point the world becomes hard and unyielding. We stub our toes in the dark and corrode our livers with alcohol. If, while maneuvering in a high place, we cease paying attention and try to become free spirits, we are likely to fall and break our necks. We have hardly any alternative to submitting to the laws of nature. In the second place, we cannot give unbridled freedom to our desires because we will conflicting things. We will both to eat a lot and remain trim. We will both to indulge our temper and to keep our friends. We will to have our cake and eat it too.

Since we will conflicting things, we are forced to make value judgments. We are forced to consider exactly what it is we prefer. This is true even on the level of simple prudence. Apart from any idea of good or evil in the moral sense, we must consider which of two incompatible pleasures we value most. If we do not yield ourselves over to the sheerest indulgence, if we exercise any foresight at all, we find ourselves submitting to the authority of the laws of nature.

Submitting to the laws of nature, as with nearly all submission, is a matter of degrees. At one end of the spectrum we read of very young members of street gangs in New York City who indulge every appetite the moment it makes itself felt. Those that survive the gang fights soon find their health giving way under the burden of narcotic poisoning and venereal disease. Their manner of life is so indulgent and corrupt it is barely compatible with the sustenance of life itself, and that only for a relatively short time. Higher up on the scale we may observe the sophisticated criminal. He submits himself readily enough to the physical and biological laws which make life and health and work possible. He may, indeed, exercise remarkable self-discipline in conforming his work habits and plans of action to the necessities imposed upon him by the physical world. He may even scrupulously submit himself to the laws of the land insofar as those laws cannot be evaded or where the risk of being caught makes the payoff not worthwhile. In principle, the successful criminal knows the meaning of authority. Authority is that to which we must or should submit our will.

The submission of our will, our ego, our pride is a fundamental necessity of life. To whatever extent life as a "free spirit" is possible – and it is possible to a great extent – that life can only be experienced *after* one has learned obedience. Undisciplined freedom is impossible. No serious thinker has thought otherwise. No one has ever experienced life on any other principle. The submission of the will is man's hardest, most utterly disagreeable task. Men may be gods, but no man is God. No man's will is sovereign. Whatever else man may be, he is a creature. No king on his throne is immune to these fundamental truths.

Some authority is by fact, some is by right, and some is both. The authority of the laws of nature over our bodies is an example of the authority of fact. Other fundamental examples of the authority of fact. (i.e., brute force) are the authority of the government over its citizens (which authority may also be by right) and the authority of parents over small children (usually also by right). Examples of "forces" or "realities" which have rightful authority over us, but not necessarily effectual authority, are the authority of reason, of conscience, and of the aesthetic sensitivity. Men ought to be reasonable, moral, sensitive, but need not be.

Here we obviously face the problem of ethics in general. Does man face *any* real ought? If so, why? *De facto* authority is something we either recognize and submit to or we pay the penalty for our disobedience right quickly. It is still an open question whether we *ought* always to submit to *de facto* authority. (There are probably few if any occasions on which we ought to resist the *de facto* authority which nature has over our bodies. We do sometimes feel, as sentient, rational creatures, as budding free spirits, that we ought not be bound by the crude, brute laws of nature. Ultimately, that feeling may be valid. But the proof of such an esoteric proposition would be highly metaphysical and delicate.) In any case, as soon as we go beyond *de facto* authority to which we either must submit or ought to submit for prudential reasons, we must face the question of whether we have a *moral* obligation to submit ourselves to any authority whatever.

As a philosopher I am very sorry to have to confess that I can see no way of grounding the moral good other than in God. True enough, man has a deeply felt value sense, but if this feeling is not grounded in the fact of God's valuing of us, then I can see no way of justifying the claims this feeling makes on us. With many skeptics through the ages, we should then have to say the conscience is illusion, or the tool of the strong to suppress the weak (or, as in Nietzsche, the tool of the weak to suppress the strong). If anyone can clearly show why men ought to be moral, other than for prudential reasons, I would gladly see the demonstration. I am eager to believe that good has its basis in nature apart from the question of God's existence. But how blind nature can justify my feeling that man is valuable, more valuable than a virus or a rock or indeed more valuable than empty space, I cannot see. Thus I am driven to conclude that all authority of right has its roots in God's valuing of men and in His will generally.[1]

If morality is grounded only upon expedience or prudence, the very strong or powerful man need only submit to the physical laws of nature: he may then impose his will upon other men in any fashion he chooses for his might is his right. He is in the position of the king in Hobbes' *Leviathan*. I doubt if any man can, in clear language and with reasoning transparent to the normal intelligence, show otherwise. Even if we show that the lawless man will ruin his own happiness, there is no proof that he *ought* to will his own happiness, nor is there proof that men even know what their own happiness is or that they unambiguously will it when they think they know it or that it is the same for each man. Without value grounded in God, man is an empty passion, nothing more.

Man is a lawless rebel. He rebels against the holiness of God. He rebels with resentments, murders, and slaughters against his fellow man. Man is even a rebel against the laws of nature (alchemy, magic).

[1] It is beyond our present purposes to argue the question of God's existence, or carefully to explore the implications for ethics if we assume His non-existence. For the present essay we will assume God's existence, or at least assume some satisfactory answer to the question, "Why should I be moral?"

Science represents man's grudging discovery that he must submit himself to nature's laws, and *by submitting*, free himself. The parallel in other areas of life, unfortunately, holds. Man only conquers by yielding. "Resist not evil." "Turn the other cheek." "Submit yourself to God." "Overcome evil with good." These things are hard to believe, but all these lessons are found in principle in man's scientific experience. Man overcomes nature by submitting and resisting not. The lessons are universally applicable. That is, they are applicable not only to our dealings with nature but also to our dealings with men and God.

Government and the submission to a common law are quite evidently the necessary prerequisites to social freedom.[2] The more generously the authority of a government is acknowledged, the more openness and freedom may manifest themselves in the social life. The more a people resist their government, the more defensive and repressive that government tends to become. As a rule, the more a man stiffens himself against authority, the more intractable that authority becomes. This is why a lawless people will have a tyrannical government, although the converse does not necessarily hold.

I am hard pressed to believe even in the right to revolution, as much as I would like to. The revolutionary temper is exceedingly dangerous to the man who holds it, for the spirit of rebellion is hard to control. I realize that some governments are so evil that they have likely forfeited any right to govern.[3] But whether we have the right to kill the men constituting those governments on that account is something not at all clear to me. Few consider to try to overcome evil with good. Little imagination goes into thinking of ways to accomplish this and little work into the effort. If the days come when men learn the true laws of human nature, revolution may appear as barbarous, uneconomic, and wicked as slavery and human sacrifice seem now.

In every affair of life, from the greatest to the least, men must stoop to conquer. This truth pleases me as little as it pleases any man. Stooping is backbreaking labor. The will, the ego, the pride are involved. The self wishes to exert itself, expand itself, reign supreme. Sartre is not wrong when he says each man wishes to be God. But no man is God, and the most fundamental lesson that life has to teach a man is

---

[2] Animal studies show in many cases a pecking order. Even in the primitive animal society the necessity for anthority is thus apparently found.

[3] In general not all authorities should be submitted to. Some authorities have precedence over others, and one mnst also note pretended authority. This last proviso shows the ultimate authority of the individual conscience, inasmuch as each man must judge for himself that to which he ought to submit.

that very fact, that man is a creature, of limited power, limited vision, and that until he learns his place as a creature he will only kick against the goads, but that when he learns his role and accepts it in an act of submission he may become a god.

The dissolving of the ego and the partial blending of one's self with others is what love is about. There can be no true love, only selfish passion, where the laws of love are not submitted to. Those laws are the laws of submitting to the legitimate will of the beloved, i.e., permitting the other person his full measure of freedom and not seeking to consume his being in possessive love. We may possess only by turning loose.

Having said this much in favor of submission and the restraint of the will, I should like to say something on the other side. There is a deep instinct in man that speaks to him of his value, that tells him he has the right to be a king, that calls upon him to live on a high plane of freedom and ecstasy. This is why men so deeply resent servitude and oppression, why men resent the necessity for discipline and self-control, why men feel that the circumstances of life have unfairly hindered the full expression of all their glorious potentials. This instinct which speaks to us of freedom and sovereignty is a true instinct. We must indeed have the courage to believe it and we must resist the tendency toward doubt and cynicism. The humanists and the theists alike perceive that somehow man has a high and resplendent destiny.

In moments of high creativity, in love, and in worship men get a glimpse of what they take to be their rightful inheritance. Unfortunately many people come back from these tastes of joy only the more resentful of everything in life that appears to hold them down and resist their will. Thus they come to resist all authority, falsely imagining that the submission of their will is incompatible with freedom and ecstasy. On the contrary, however, the submission of the will is a necessary precondition of ecstasy, and especially so of any joy that lasts beyond the moment and leaves no bitter aftertaste.

I am not pleased that these remarks have the flavor of a sermon. But it is a fact that all of the great religions emphasize the discipline of the self, and this emphasis rests upon most clearly apprehended insights into the nature of man. The philosophers are at fault if they have not spoken clearly of these truths.

One final word: ethical difficulties are predominately practical, not theoretical. Both practically and theoretically the difficulties are enormous. But given the sense of ought which we all have, we are faced with the extreme difficulty of obeying it. We know far more good than we practice. This includes people – it *especially* includes people who try to live right, for only they know how desperately the flesh lusteth against the spirit and the spirit against the flesh, how, in spite of all resolutions and resistances of the will, evil comes out. Thus, it is one thing to recognize the need and necessity of submitting the will to the perceived good and another thing altogether to find the strength to do so. Here again the philosophers often show themselves very shallow. They often write as if to know the good is to be empowered to do the good. More realistic, perhaps, at least in this respect, are the determinists who speak of the bondage of the will. Without acknowledging the truth of determinism, it is well to note that men sometimes find it nearly impossible to do the good they desire. This fact drives some Christians to say that obedience to God is itself a gift of God. Whether that is true or not I do not know, but as an answer it has the merit of recognizing in its fulness the difficulty and the mystery of submission.

To review: Authority is whatever must or should be submitted to. Many things must be submitted to but the only thing that ought to be submitted to is God's will. All value stems from God and all values, in their proper place, have authority over us. Moreover, the necessity of submission is fundamental to the human condition. Men have unlimited desires and pretensions, but, of themselves, only limited powers and means. By bending the ego to God, we come at last to partake of His glory and power. By bending the ego to science we come to partake in the power of nature's laws. By bending the ego to our neighbor we come to drink deep of love. Man's raw, unrestrained ego must be humbled, although there are a thousand ways of seeming to humble it while only exalting it ("though I give my body to be burned," etc.). When the ego is submitted and disciplined, it is capable of loving, i.e., blending with other egos, including God's. It is then capable of ecstasy. The unrestrained ego can never get out of itself: a dark prison indeed. To leave the prison of one's ego, one must yield some autonomy over to the legitimate will of others, particularly to the will of that Other who offers to man His unlimited power and splendor. Man is under the grim necessity of abandoning his impossible pretensions and bending his restless ego to that only Source of freedom, light, and joy. Only by bending, submitting, does man loose himself from his chains and become free to soar.

AN ANALYSIS OF AUTHORITY

J. M. Bochenski O.P.

The aim of the present paper is to restate and expand upon some of the statements made in a previous study* of some of the basic aspects of authority. Special attention has been paid here to deontic authority, which was hardly analyzed at all in the previous study.

What is offered here is an analysis which is, in most cases, purely logical, more exactly pragmatic, but conducted with formal logical tools. However, a few empirical assumptions are made in §§ 4 and 9. Those assumptions are valid only where *human* authority is concerned; consequently, the portions of our study based on them deal with that authority alone. On the other hand, whatever is not based on those assumptions applies to all possible entities, i.e., to God also. A theory of every possible authority is constructed. This applies to all theorems, with the exception of some which appear under §§ 4 and 9.

An elementary logical apparatus is used throughout, taken mostly from *Principia Mathematica*. However, as usually happens when a concrete philosophical problematic is treated, some parts of formal logic had to be established for the sake of this study.

Together with logical symbols, a number of extralogical constants are employed. Among them the following appear more frequently:

"$A(x, y, \gamma)$" for "x is an authority to y in the field γ"
"$AC(x, p)$" for "x accepts p"
"$CO(x, p, y)$" for "x communicates p to y with assertion"
"$DA(x, y, \gamma)$" for "x is a deontic authority to y in the field γ"
"$DS(x, p)$" for "x desires that p"
"$EA(x, y, \gamma)$" for "x is an epistemic authority to y in the field γ"
"$Pr(p, x, t)$" for "the probability of p as related to the state of knowledge of x at the time t."

---

* *The Logic of Religion*, New York University Press, N.Y., 1965, pp. 162–173.

I. FUNDAMENTAL STRUCTURE

The term "authority" is used mostly as a substantive or as an adjective, e.g., in phrases such as "x is a great authority" or "x possesses considerable authority." In this respect it is similar to terms such as "neighbor," "father," "friend." Even a superficial analysis shows, however, that the concepts symbolized by such terms can be analysed into concepts of relations, but not inversely. In other words, the basic structure of what is meant by these terms is a relation. This is true also of "authority."

1.1 Elementary Analysis

Authority is a ternary (triadic) *relation.* It is a relation holding between several terms; there are always three such terms. Whenever there is authority the following situation occurs: first, there is someone, x, who is said to have authority; reference will here be made to "the bearer" of authority. Second, there is someone, y, for whom the bearer is an authority; this will be referred to as "the subject." Finally, there is a class of entities, γ, to be referred to as "the field," in which x has authority for y. The following is an example: James, a professor of logic, is an authority for John, a student, in the field of logic. James is the bearer, John the subject, and the class of logical laws and rules the field of authority.

We shall symbolize "x has authority for y in γ" by

$$A(x, y, \gamma).$$

The following remarks are of importance:

(1) *The bearer and the subject of authority are individuals.* One often speaks, it is true, of the authority of a class of persons, e.g. of the class of physicians, and also of someone's authority for a group of men, e.g., the authority of a captain over the company. It is, however, easy to show that these, let us say, group-authorities can be analysed in terms of individual bearers and subjects.

(2) *The bearer and the subject of authority are conscious beings.* We could even say that they are rational beings or persons, and we shall assume that in most cases they are. However, as not every authority is rational – the case among certain animals – the weaker statement will be retained.

As far as the third term of A is concerned, a linguistic difficulty arises due to the lack of a convenient English word. The following can be said about it:

(3) *The field is not a class of utterances, but of what utterances mean*, in other words, a class of meanings. These meanings must be communicated by utterances. Yet authority is not about utterances, but about what they mean.[1]

(4) *It is a class of complete meanings*, i.e., such as may be communicated autonomously and not only in the context of wider meanings. Such are propositions and rules.

(5) *It is always a class* with several elements. It seems essential that authority should be about a whole class and not only about one single entity.

1.2 Definition

Authority need not be a primitive term: it can be defined by simpler terms, viz. the expressions "communicates with assertion" and "accepts as valid". Whenever we have $A(x, y, \gamma)$ we also have the following situation: if x communicates to y with assertion an element of γ, y accepts it as valid. And inversely: if the latter is the case, we have $A(x, y, \gamma)$. We put "$CO(x, y, p)$" for "x communicates p with assertion to y" and "$AC(y, p)$ for "y accepts p as valid". We can then write:

1.21 $\quad A(x, y, \gamma) :\equiv: (p) : p \in \gamma . CO(x, y, p) . \supset . AC(y, p).$*

The negation of 1.21 is of interest:

1.22 $\quad \sim A(x, y, \gamma) :\equiv: (\exists p) . p \in \gamma . CO(x, y, p) . \sim AC(y, p),$

i.e., x is not an authority to y in γ, if and only if there is at least one p belonging to γ and communicated by x to y with assertion but not accepted by y.

It may be objected against 1.21 that the acceptance of all utterances communicated by the authority and belonging to the field is not a necessary condition of authority. It happens, as a matter of fact, that $A(x, y, \gamma)$ and yet there is at least one p belonging to γ and communicated by x to y which is not accepted by y. E.g., it happens that

---

[1] While this is not the place to discuss the problem of the existence of meanings, it may be stressed that those who deny it would have considerable difficulty in formulating a theory of authority.

* The difficulty involved in all definitions of habitual properties also occurs here and in similar cases. It is disregarded for the sake of simplicity.

a student does not accept something the professor communicates in his own field, in a case, say, where he commits an obvious error in writing on the blackboard.

However, this is not a fatal objection to 1.21. The only thing that it shows is that there are exceptions. But exceptions always occur in human affairs. It is true that in order to be quite precise we should add a phrase such as "as a general rule" or something similar. This phrase is presupposed here and in what follows.

1.3 Use and misuse of authority

x is said to use his authority in regard to a subject y and a field γ if (1) $A(x, y, \gamma)$, (2) there is at least one p such that p belongs to γ and x communicates p to y with assertion. If we put "$UA(x, y, \gamma)$" for "x uses his authority in regard to y and γ" we can write:

1.31 $UA(x, y, \gamma) .\equiv. A(x, y, \gamma).(\exists p).p \in \gamma.CO(x, y, p)$.

As to the misuse of authority, two different kinds can be distinguished: one can misuse authority in regard to a field and in regard to a subject.

The first kind of misuse is present if and only if four conditions are satisfied: (1) $A(x, y, \gamma)$; (2) $\sim A(x, y, \delta)$; (3) $CO(x, y, p).p \in \delta$; (4) x suggests that because $A(x, y, \gamma)$, also $A(x, y, \delta)$.

The second kind also requires four conditions: (1) $A(x, y, \gamma)$; (2) $\sim A(x, z, \gamma)$; (3) $CO(x, z, p).p \in \gamma$; (4) x suggests that because $A(x, y, \gamma)$ also $A(x, z, \gamma)$.

The classical instance of the misuse of authority of the first kind is collective declarations by professors, usually highly competent, in certain scientific fields such as roentgenology, philosophy or biblical studies, who communicate with assertion statements belonging to politics. All conditions enumerated above are present: they are authorities in some field; they are not authorities in politics; they communicate statements belonging to politics; they claim implicitly that because they have authority in their fields they also have it in politics, which is false.

As to the third condition, it is perhaps not explicitly stated by the signatories of such declarations, but the fact that they sign collectively and with their full scientific titles cannot but make the impression that they are speaking "in the name of science," i.e., that they claim to possess authority in the field in which they are making statements – politics.[2]

2. FORMAL THEORY

A formal theory of ternary relations not being readily available, some of the chapters constituting such a theory will be sketched here.

2.1 Partial relations

Each ternary relation contains 6 partial binary relations. The first three are defined as follows:

2.1 $\quad\quad\quad A_1 =_{Df} \hat{x}\hat{y}((\exists \gamma).A(x, y, \gamma)$

2.2 $\quad\quad\quad A_2 =_{Df} \hat{x}\hat{\gamma}((\exists y).A(x, y, \gamma)$

2.3 $\quad\quad\quad A_3 =_{Df} \hat{y}\hat{\gamma}((\exists x).A(x, y, \gamma).$

A_1 is the relation which holds between the bearer and the subject; A_2 that between the bearer and the field; A_3 holds between the subject and the field. The remaining three are converses of the first three.

2.2 Domains and descriptions

There are three domains in a ternary relation and, properly speaking, no co-domains. Thus we have, e.g.:

2.21 $\quad\quad\quad D_1'A =_{Df} D'A_1$

The first domain of A is the domain of A_1, namely, the class of all bearers of authority.

There are also three ways in which a relation may be limited in its domains. Since these limitations may be accumulated, we obtain six different concepts altogether.

While there are only 6 different kinds of description by a binary relation, a ternary relation allows no less than 24. As in the case of A, however, the third argument is a class; therefore, only 12 kinds of description are relevant.

Domains, limited domains and descriptions will be only marginally

---

[2] Such a statement was published by a large group of prominent German scientists in 1914. It asserted that Germany did not attack Belgium. Among the signatories were Roentgen, Husserl and Harnack!

AN ANALYSIS OF AUTHORITY

employed in this study and are therefore not defined. Their mention only serves to emphasize the complexity of the concept of authority.

2.3 Properties of relations

The theory of the properties of ternary relations is also more complex than that of binary relations. This can be illustrated by the case of symmetry. A binary relation is symmetric or asymmetric. That is all. But a ternary relation may be symmetric, first of all, in three different ways, according to the symmetry of A_1, A_2 or A_3. Moreover, these symmetries may be accumulated and we obtain 6 different kinds altogether.

Furthermore, we may speak of symmetry with a given third term and of symmetry with all third terms of the relation. Altogether, consequently, we have 12 different concepts of symmetry and 12 of asymmetry.

In the case of A, however, the third term belongs to a higher type than the first two, so that the symmetry of A_2 and A_3 does not make sense and there are no accumulations. Thus we are left with only two different symmetries: that of all given fields and that of all fields. Similar considerations apply to reflexivity.

2.311 $\quad$ REFL$(A, \gamma) =_{Df} (x)A(x, x, \gamma)$

2.312 $\quad$ IRREFL$(A, \gamma) =_{Df} (x) \sim A(x, x, \gamma)$

2.313 $\quad$ $A \in$ grefl $=_{Df} (\gamma)$REFL(A, γ)

2.314 $\quad$ $A \in$ girrefl $=_{Df} (\gamma)$IRREFL(A, γ)

2.321 $\quad$ SYM$(A, \gamma) =_{Df} (x, y) . A(x, y, \gamma) = A(y, x, \gamma)$

2.322 $\quad$ ASSYM$(A, \gamma) =_{Df} (x, y) . A(x, y, \gamma) = \sim A(y, x, \gamma)$

2.323 $\quad$ $A \in$ gsym $=_{Df} (\gamma)$SYM(A, γ)

2.324 $\quad$ $A \in$ gassym $=_{Df} (\gamma)$ASSYM(A, γ).

As far as transitivity is concerned, the situation is still more complex. We have, first, two concepts of transitivity, analogous to those of symmetry and reflexivity:

2.331 $\quad$ TRANS$(A,\gamma) =_{Df} : (x, y) : (\exists t) . A(x, t, \gamma) . A(t, y, \gamma) . \supset . A(x, y, \gamma)$

2.332 $\quad$ INTRANS$(A,\gamma) =_{Df} : (x, y, t) : A(x, t, \gamma) . A(t, y, \gamma) . \supset . \sim A(x, y, \gamma)$

2.332 $A \in \text{gtrans} =_{Df} (\gamma)\text{TRANS}(A, \gamma)$

2.333 $A \in \text{gintrans} =_{Df} (\gamma)\text{INTRANS}(A, \gamma)$.

But there are also three other kinds of transitivity (or intransitivity), where, contrary to the above, there are two different fields:

2.334 $A \in \text{gen}_1\text{trans} =_{Df} : (x, y, \gamma_1, \gamma_2) : (\exists t) . A(x, t, \gamma_1) . A(t, y, \gamma_2) . \supset . A(x, y, \gamma_1)$

2.335 $A \in \text{gen}_2\text{trans} =_{Df} : (x, y, \gamma_1, \gamma_2) : (\exists t) . A(x, t, \gamma_1) . A(t, y, \gamma_2) . \supset . A(x, y, \gamma_2)$

2.336 $A \in \text{gen}_3\text{trans} =_{Df} : (x, y, \gamma_1, \gamma_2) : (\exists t) . A(x, t, \gamma_1) . A(t, y, \gamma_2) . \supset . A(x, y, \gamma_1) . A(x, y, \gamma_2)$

The corresponding intransitivities are:

2.337 $A \in \text{gen}_1\text{intrans} =_{Df} (x, y, \gamma_1, \gamma_2, t) . A(x, t, \gamma_1) . A(t, y, \gamma_2) . \sim A(x, y, \gamma_1)$

2.328 $A \in \text{gen}_2\text{intrans} =_{Df} (x, y, \gamma_1, \gamma_2, t) . A(x, t, \gamma_1) . A(t, y, \gamma_2) . \sim A(x, y, \gamma_2)$

2.339 $A \in \text{gen}_3\text{intrans} =_{Df} (x, y, \gamma_1, \gamma_2, t) : A(x, t, \gamma_1) . A(t, y, \gamma_2) . \sim A(x, y, \gamma_1) \vee \sim A(x, y, \gamma_2)$

2.4 Extension to classes

Relations holding between classes of each of the three terms of A can be defined. We put:

2.41 $AG_1(\alpha, x, \gamma) =_{Df} (x) . x \in \alpha \supset A(x, y, \gamma)$

2.42 $AG_2(x, \beta, \gamma) =_{Df} (y) . y \in \beta \supset A(x, y, \gamma)$

2.43 $AG_3(\alpha, \beta, \gamma) =_{Df} (x, y) : x \in \alpha . y \in \beta \supset . A(x, y, \gamma)$

A class of fields can also be constructed and three more relations of the above sort can be defined as well, but these are of lesser interest in our case.

2.41 to 2.43 show how a "social" authority can be analysed in terms of individual authority, according to the statement in #1.

2.5 Generalizations

Altogether there are 48 different generalizations of three variables with two types of quantifier. However, only 26 among them are not equivalent to any other.[3] The equivalences are obtained by use of the following rules:

R. 1. If all quantifiers are of the same type (all universal or all existential) and one follows the other immediately, their order may be changed.

R. 2. A universal quantifier may be replaced by an existential quantifier.

R. 3. In a group of quantifiers an existential quantifier may be moved to the *right*.

The non-equivalent generalizations are listed in the following table, where the matrix "A(x, y, γ)" has been omitted and the implicators are indicated by arrows.[4]

---

[3] The corresponding statement in the *Logic of Religion* (p. 163) is incorrect.
[4] The full table of quantifiers which may be attached to the matrix "A(x, y, γ)" is:

	a	b	c	d	e	f
(1)	(x, y, γ)	(x, γ, y)	(y, x, γ)	(y, γ, x)	(γ, x, y)	(γ, y, x)
(2)	(x, y)(∃γ)	(x)(∃γ)(y)	(y, x)(∃γ)	(y)(∃γ)(x)	(∃γ)(x, y)	(∃γ)(y, x)
(3)	(x)(∃y)(γ)	(x, γ)(∃y)	(∃y)(x, γ)	(∃y)(γ, x)	(γ, x)(∃y)	(γ)(∃y)(x)
(4)	(x)(∃y, γ)	(x)(∃γ, y)	(∃y)(x)(∃γ)	(∃y, γ)(x)	(∃γ)(x)(∃y)	(∃γ, y)(x)
(5)	(∃x)(y, γ)	(∃x)(γ, y)	(y)(∃x)(γ)	(y, γ)(∃x)	(γ)(∃x)(y)	(γ, y)(∃x)
(6)	(∃x)(y)(∃γ)	(∃x, γ)(y)	(y)(∃x, γ)	(y)(∃γ, x)	(∃γ,x)(y)	(∃γ)(y)(∃x)
(7)	(∃x, y)(γ)	(∃x) (γ)(Ey)	(∃y, x)(γ)	(∃y)(γ)(∃x)	(γ)(∃x, y)	(γ)(∃y, x)
(8)	(∃x, y, γ)	(∃x, γ, y)	(∃y, x, γ)	(∃y, γ, x)	(∃γ, x, y)	(∃γ, y, x)

Applying R1 twice, we obtain the following equivalences (the formulae are indicated by the line and the column in the above table):

(1)	all in line 1:		1
(2)	a ≡ c and e ≡ f in 2 and 7:	4 + 4	8
(3)	b ≡ e and c ≡ d in 3 and 6:	4 + 4	8
(4)	a ≡ b and d ≡ f in 4 and 5:	4 + 4	8
(5)	all in 8:		1
			26

(The figures on the right indicate the number of non-equivalent formulae).

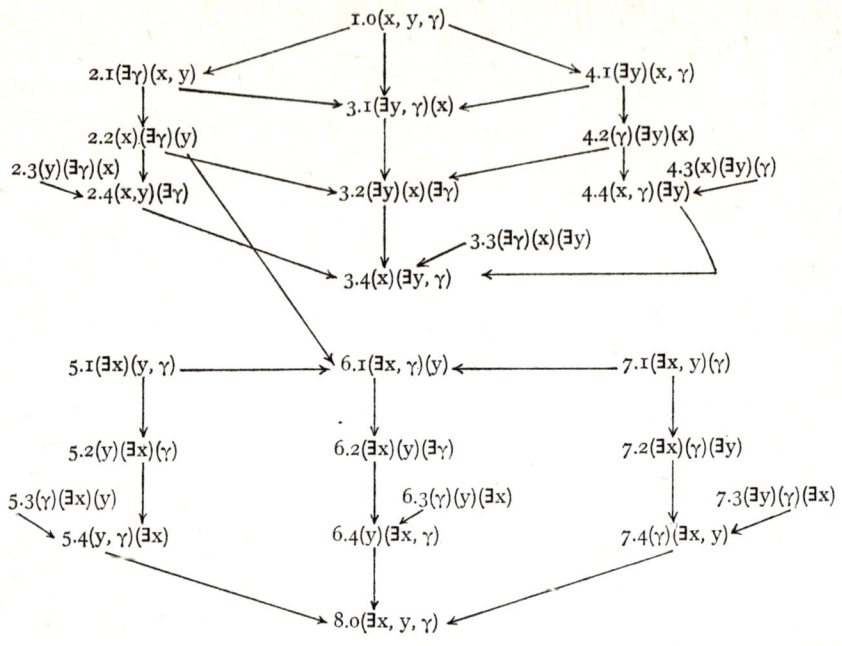

3. BASIC THEOREMS

In this chapter three basic theorems on authority in general will be stated. They are all based on the current understanding of the expression "authority" as analysed in § 1.

3.1 Irreflexivity

3.11 $\qquad$ A ∈ girrefl.

In view of the definition 2.314, this means:

3.12 $\qquad$ (x, γ). ∼A(x, x, γ):

Nobody is an authority for himself in any field.

3.13 $\qquad$ (x, y, γ).x = y ⊃ ∼A(x, y, γ).

This theorem could be challenged through use of the term in the following way. It happens, that someone who wrote a book on mathematical logic consults it several years later in order to see if a theorem is true; one would then be tempted to say that he is an authority for himself. However, if the expression "himself" is sufficiently analysed, it does not appear to be inconsistent with 3.11. For the author of the book at the time of writing is one individual, while the same author several years later is another, as can be seen by the fact that the first knows something the second does not.

3.2 Asymmetry

3.21 $\qquad A \in \text{gass}$

Because of 2.324 and 2.322, this is equivalent to:

3.22 $\qquad (x, y, \gamma) . A(x, y, \gamma) . \supset . \sim A(y, x, \gamma).$

If x is an authority for y in γ, y is not an authority for x in the same field – this for all bearers, subjects, and fields. This important theorem will be referred to as "Ass," "the principle of asymmetry." It may be noted that a much stronger formula, viz.:

$$(x, y) . A_1(x, y) . \supset \sim A_1(y, x)$$

does *not* hold. In fact, there is no apparent inconsistency in:

$$(\exists x, y) . A_1(x, y) . A_1(y, x),$$

which can be seen by substituting the respective definitions for both arguments; as a result we obtain:

$$(\exists x, y) . (\exists \gamma) A(x, y, \gamma) . (\exists \gamma) A(y, x, \gamma)$$

where both γ are different. In this case x is an authority for y in one field and y for x in another, which is not only logically possible but often a fact. Thus to cite just one instance, the professor is an authority in logic for a certain student who, at the same time, is an authority for the professor as far as the technique of soaring is concerned.

One obvious, but technically relevant, consequence of 3.2 is:

3.23 $\qquad (x, y) . A_1(x, y) \supset x \neq y:$

if x is the authority for y, then x is not identical with y.

3.3 Transitivity

3.31 $\qquad A \in \text{gtrans},$

which, in view of 2.343, is equivalent to:

3.32 $\quad (x, y, \gamma) : (\exists t) . A(x, t, \gamma) . A(t, y, \gamma) . \supset . A(x, y, \gamma).$

The authority of an authority in the same field is an authority. If x is an authority for t and t is an authority for y in γ, then x is also an authority for y in γ. E.g., let x be a university professor of English, and t, his student; and let t be the teacher of a child y in grade school. According to the theorem x will be an authority for y in English.

On the other hand, there is no transitivity when the fields are different. Consequently we have:

3.33 $\qquad\qquad A\sim \in \text{gen}_1\text{trans}$

3.34 $\qquad\qquad A\sim \in \text{gen}_2\text{trans}$

3.35 $\qquad\qquad A\sim \in \text{gen}_3\text{trans}$

which does not imply that authority is intransitive in the same way. Let x be a university professor of English, t his student, and y a pupil of t in music. It may happen that y is as well or better versed in English than x and, thus, that x is not an authority for him in that field. He is also not an authority in music and, *a fortiori*, in both fields. Or, let x be the head of the tax-office, t a tax-payer, and let the same t be a company commander, while y is a member of his company. x need not be an authority to y either in the field of the rules concerning tax-paying, or in that of military rules. It may even happen, that x is himself a member of the company and, thus, far from being an authority for y in the field of military rules, may be the subject of authority (if y is, e.g., his sergeant).

4. THE EXISTENCE OF AUTHORITY

In this chapter a number of theorems will be stated concerning the existence of certain authorities in general. Contrary to those formulated in chapter 3, they are all based on experience and cannot be obtained by linguistic analysis alone. However, the acceptance of only one theorem directly based on experience is necessary since a large number of other theorems is implied by it in the framework of the basic ones.

4.1 Axiom

Everyone is an authority in at least one field for everyone else.

4.11 $\qquad (x)(\exists\gamma)(y)\ x \neq y \supset A(x, y, \gamma).$

This can be shown in the following way. Let x be a child and γ the class of propositions concerning his stomach pains. It should be evident that the child knows better about those pains than anyone else, i.e., that he is an authority for everyone else in this field. Let "a" be an abbreviation for the child's name, "ϑ" for the particular class of propositions; we have then:

(1) $\qquad (y).y \neq a \supset A(a, y, \vartheta).$

From (1) we obtain by elementary logic:

(2) $\qquad (\exists x, \gamma)(y).y \neq x \supset A(x, y, \gamma).$

Moreover, if the child has been chosen due to the fact that it represents, so to speak, the minimum of authority, we can generalize and state that the same is true about all of our own stomach pains, about all of our personal feelings. This yields:

(3) $\qquad (x)(\exists\gamma)(y)\ A(x, y, \gamma).$

However, (3) cannot be accepted as a correct formulation because of 3.12. We must therefore add the condition of non-identity to (3) and write:

(4) $\qquad (x)(\exists\gamma)(y).x \neq y \supset A(x, y, \gamma)$

which is 4.11 and (2.2).

4.2 First-level theorems

4.11 entails a number of theorems:

4.21 (2.4)	$(x, y)(\exists\gamma).x \neq y \supset A(x, y, \gamma)$	by 4.11
4.22 (3.2)	$(\exists y)(x)(\exists\gamma).x \neq y \supset A(x, y, \gamma)$	by 4.11
4.23 (3.4)	$(x)(\exists y, \gamma).x \neq y \supset A(x, y, \gamma)$	by 4.22
4.24 (6.1)	$(\exists x, \gamma)(y).x \neq y \supset A(x, y, \gamma)$	by 4.11
4.25 (6.2)	$(\exists x)(y)(\exists\gamma).x \neq y \supset A(x, y, \gamma)$	by 4.24

4.26 (6.4) $(y)(\exists x, \gamma) . x \neq y \supset A(x, y, \gamma)$ by 4.25

4.27 (8.0) $(\exists x, y, \gamma) . x \neq y \supset A(x, y, \gamma)$ by 4.21, 4.23 or 4.25.

4.3 Second-level theorems

From these a number of further theorems can be obtained with the principle of asymmetry. Here we shall give the proof only of the first, the others being quite similar.

(1) $(x, y, \gamma) . A(x, y, \gamma) \supset \sim A(y, x, \gamma)$ (Ass.)

(2) $(x, \gamma, y) . A(x, y, \gamma) \supset \sim A(y, x, \gamma)$ (R. 1.)

(3) $(x)(\exists \gamma)(y) : x \neq y . \supset A(x, y, \gamma)$ (4.11)

(4) $(x)(\exists \gamma)(y) : x \neq y . \supset \sim A(y, x, \gamma)$ (by (2) and (3))

(5) $(y)(\exists \gamma)(x) : y \neq x . \supset \sim A(x, y, \gamma)$ (by transliteration)

(6) $(y)(\exists \gamma)(x) : x \neq y . \supset \sim A(x, y, \gamma)$ (by symmetry of $\neq$)

(7) $(y)(\exists \gamma)(x) \sim A(x, y, \gamma)$ (by (6) and 3.13).

Each of the theorems thus obtained is the equivalent of the negation of one of the formulas in the table. The theorems and the formulas they contradict are listed below. The negations of the theorems are obtained by the following steps (for 4.21):

$$\sim(y)(\exists \gamma)(x) \sim A(x, y, \gamma)$$

$$(\exists y)(\gamma)(\exists x) \sim\sim A(x, y, \gamma)$$

$$(\exists y)(\gamma)(\exists x) A(x, y, \gamma)$$

4.31	$(y)(\exists \gamma)(x) . \sim A(x, y, \gamma)$	(7.3)	$(\exists y)(\gamma)(\exists x) . A(x, y, \gamma)$
4.32	$(x, y)(\exists \gamma) . \sim A(x, y, \gamma)$	(7.1)	$(\exists x, y)(\gamma) . A(x, y, \gamma)$
4.33	$(\exists x)(y)(\exists \gamma) . \sim A(x, y, \gamma)$	(4.3)	$(x)(\exists y)(\gamma) . A(x, y, \gamma)$
4.34	$(y)(\exists x, \gamma) . \sim A(x, y, \gamma)$	(3.4)	$(\exists y)(x, \gamma) . A(x, y, \gamma)$
4.35	$(\exists y, \gamma)(x) . \sim A(x, y, \gamma)$	(5.4)	$(y, \gamma)(\exists x) . A(x, y, \gamma)$
4.36	$(\exists y)(x)(\exists \gamma) . \sim A(x, y, \gamma)$	(5.2)	$(y)(\exists x)(\gamma) . A(x, y, \gamma)$
4.37	$(x)(\exists y, \gamma) . \sim A(x, y, \gamma)$	(5.1)	$(\exists x)(y, \gamma) . A(x, y, \gamma)$
4.38	$(\exists x, y, \gamma) . \sim A(x, y, \gamma)$	(1.0)	$(x, y, \gamma) . A(x, y, \gamma)$

AN ANALYSIS OF AUTHORITY

The formulas on the left are all true; those on the right all false. Consequently, the truth-value of $8 + 8 = 16$ out of 26 formulas has been established.

The main results of this analysis are: first, there is no "absolute" human authority. However large its field may be, there is always a set of propositions or rules which do not belong to it. Second, the problem of the existence of "authority" is highly complex. This fact seems to be frequently disregarded by people who call themselves "anti-authoritarians".

4.4 On Anti-authoritarianism

Those who call themselves "anti-authoritarians" seem to claim, as an ideal, the existence of a state in which there would be no authority at all. What is more, when asked why they consider such an ideal, they respond that this is because every authority is "illegitimate." Now, in this context "illegitimate" must mean "non-existent." Basically, what they mean, then, is that there *is* no authority, but only apparent authority.

If taken literally, that claim is equivalent to the contention that 4.28 does not hold, i.e., that:

(1) $\qquad \sim (\exists x, y, \gamma) . A(x, y, \gamma)$

which is equivalent to:

(2) $\qquad (x, y, \gamma) \sim A(x, y, \gamma).$

But (2) is quite obviously false and therefore cannot be what the anti-authoritarians mean. On the other hand, they do not seem to deny:

(3) $\qquad (x, y, \gamma) . A(x, y, \gamma)$

i.e., to assert theorem 4.28:

$$(\exists x, y, \gamma) . \sim A(x, y, \gamma),$$

for this is obviously true and need not be propagandized in any way.

It seems to follow that they reject one of the intermediary formulas. But since there are no less than 24 of these it is difficult to decide which it is exactly that is meant, all the more since the analysis developed up to now is quite general and does not take into consideration the refinements needed to deal with different kinds of authority.

In point of fact, the hypothesis that the anti-authoritarians mean only one of the several kinds of authority, is plausible. The problem will be treated in a more detailed manner below.

4.5 On Divine Authority

4.11 is true only if the first and second domains of authority are limited to finite being, i.e., if all bearers and subjects are assumed to be such beings. For let g be an infinite being, endowed with infinite knowledge and conceived as a universal leader, then the following statement will apply:

4.51 $$(y, \gamma) : y \neq g . \supset . A(g, y, \gamma).$$

That is, g is an authority for all beings different from it in all fields. With the principle of asymmetry, this entails:

4.52 $$(x, \gamma) : x \neq g . \supset . \sim A(x, g, \gamma):$$

no being different from g is an authority for g in any field. Consequently,

$$(x)(\exists \gamma) : x \neq g . \supset . A(x, g, \gamma),$$

which is entailed by 4.11, does not hold. That being the case, several other theorems in this chapter also fall away.

An incidental result of the above is that God could be defined by authority as follows:

4.53 $$g =_{Df} (\iota x)\{(y, \gamma) : y \neq g . \supset . A(g, y, \gamma)\}.$$

God is that entity which is an authority in all fields for all subjects different from Him.

5. THE TWO KINDS OF AUTHORITY

Up to now, authority was considered in general, in so far as the nature of its field was not specified. The scope of the present chapter is to introduce and discuss distinctions in the field.

5.1 Epistemic and deontic authority

A field of authority is two-fold: it is either a class of *propositions* which state what *is*, or a class of *rules*, prescribing what *should be done*. The term "rule" is used here in a very broad way, covering the various kinds recently distinguished by students of normative logic (rules, imperatives, etc.).

If the field is a class of propositions, then the authority is that of one who knows better, i.e., of the expert in the field. This sort of authority will be called "epistemic authority." If, on the other hand, the field is a class of rules, the authority is that of a superior, a leader, a commander, etc., and will be called "deontic authority." We shall use as abbreviations "EA" and "DA" respectively.[5]

Technically speaking, epistemic authority is authority limited in its third domain to the class of propositions, while deontic authority is limited to the class of rules. This distinction seems to be exhaustive; i.e., it appears that there is no third kind of authority:

Every authority is either an epistemic or a deontic authority.

5.11 $(x, y, \gamma) : A(x, y, \gamma) . \supset . EA(x, y, \gamma) \lor DA(x, y, \gamma)$.

5.2 *The concept of coincidence*

In the above, "either-or" is taken in the non-exclusive sense, as the interpretation by "$\lor$" shows; it often happens that the same person is both an epistemic and a deontic authority for the same subject in the same field. For example, in the eyes of her small child, the mother enjoys both kinds of authority in a very wide field.

This statement needs clarification. A proposition is not a rule. Consequently, it makes no sense to say that x is both an epistemic and a deontic authority to y in the *same* field. The product of both fields is empty. What is meant by such statements is rather this: x is a deontic authority in a field γ and also an epistemic authority in regard to a class of propositions which in some way correspond to the elements of γ. Such a class is easily found for each class of rules: viz., it is that of practical propositions of the same content as the rules in question. For example, when a military commander utters the command: "fire gun no. 1" (which expresses a rule) there is a corresponding practical proposition expressed by the sentence: "it is useful for the purpose of the war to fire gun no. 1".

We can now define more precisely what we mean by the coincidence

---

[5] This distinction was made, as far as is known, for the first time in the study of 1965. It might be of interest to know that the author discovered it simply by analysing the concept of authority with logical tools, viz., after having discovered that the third term of "authority" is the name of a field, i.e., of a class, he asked himself: a class of what? This illustrates the fruitfulness of logical analysis performed with formal tools.

of both kinds of authority. We say that a bearer x is both an epistemic and a deontic authority for a subject y in a field γ, i.e., both authorities coincide, if and only if, x is a deontic authority to y in γ, and ϑ is the class of propositions corresponding to the elements of γ, then x is also an epistemic authority to y in ϑ and inversely.

By writing "CR(ϑ, γ)" for "ϑ corresponds to γ" we can formulate the definiens as follows:

$$(\gamma, \vartheta) : CR(\vartheta, \gamma) . \supset . EA(x, y, \vartheta) \equiv DA(x, y, \gamma).$$

5.3 Theorems on coincidence

In this domain there are two important empirical theorems: *Epistemic and deontic authority sometimes coincide.*

5.31 $\quad (\exists x, y, \gamma, \vartheta) . CR(\vartheta, \gamma) . EA(x, y, \gamma) \equiv DA(x, y, \vartheta).$

This is even a frequent occurrence. For example, the professor, who is primarily an epistemic authority for the student, is, at the same time, a deontic authority in the field of rules concerning the operations in the lab. So also the military commander, who is primarily a deontic authority, is (or is supposed to be in normal cases) an epistemic authority in the field of practical propositions concerning operations.

5.21 $\quad (\exists x, y, \gamma, \vartheta) : CR(\gamma, \vartheta) . EA(x, y, \gamma) . {\sim} DA(x, y, \vartheta)$

5.22 $\quad (\exists x, y, \gamma, \vartheta) : CR(\gamma, \vartheta) . {\sim} EA(x, y, \gamma) . DA(x, y, \vartheta).$

There are cases where deontic authority and epistemic authority do not coincide.

5.21 is illustrated by the case of an judicial expert. He is an expert and consequently an epistemic authority in his field. However, he is not a deontic authority in the corresponding rules of behavior for judges.

5.22 is illustrated by the case of the intelligent lieutenant standing under the command of a very un-intelligent and misinformed major. The latter is not an epistemic authority for the lieutenant in the field of propositions concerning operations; and yet he is his deontic authority in the field of corresponding commands.

This theorem is important since its negation seems to be frequently assumed. More precisely, it appears in a form such as the following:

$$(x, y, \gamma, \vartheta) : CR(\vartheta, \gamma) . \supset . DA(x, y, \vartheta) \supset EA(x, y, \gamma)$$

or, more colloquially, whoever is a deontic authority is also an epistemic authority. This seems to be assumed not only by certain individuals, but even by large social bodies such as the Communist parties in power.

5.4 Application of basic theorems

It will be clear that what was said above about the fundamental structure (§ 1) and the basic theorems (§ 3) concerning authority in general also applies to each kind of authority. Both epistemic and deontic authority are asymmetric, etc. Furthermore, what was stated about the use and abuse of authority holds for each kind. On the contrary, the existential theorems (§ 4) cannot be directly applied to both kinds. This is due to theorem 4.11, from which the others are deduced, and where the field-variable γ is bound by an existential quantifier.

Whenever a theorem holds for both kinds of authority, "EA" or "DA" may be substituted for "A."

6. EPISTEMIC AUTHORITY

6.1 Definition

The analysis of authority in general, formulated in § 1, can be extended to the two kinds of authority we have distinguished. As far as epistemic authority is concerned, the following situation is encountered. At a time t_1 the state of knowledge of the subject is s_1; and, as related to s_1, a certain proposition p has a probability m. Then at a later time t_2, the bearer of authority communicates p with assertion to the subject. The latter's state of knowledge is now enlarged by the proposition stating that the bearer communicated the proposition p; it is s_2. As related to s_2 the probability of "p" is n, where n is larger than m. The probability of "p" increased.

It is easy to see now, that wherever this is true of all propositions belonging to a field, the bearer is an authority for the subject in the field. And, inversely, whenever x is an authority for him in a certain field, this will apply to every proposition belonging to that field. There is, consequently, an equivalence between the generalization of the situation described above and the existence of authority. That being the case, this generalization can be taken as the definition of epistemic authority.

We write "$BF(t_1, t_2)$" for "t_1 is before t_2"; "$Pr(p, y, t_1)$" for "the probability of 'p' as related to the state of knowledge of y at t_1"; "$CO(x, y, p, t_2)$" for "x communicates with assertion to y the proposition p at the moment t_2". The following definition can now be formulated:

6.11
$$EA(x, y, \gamma) \equiv :(p, t_1, t_2)(\exists m, n): p \in \gamma.$$
$$BF(t_1, t_2) . Pr(p, y, t_1) = m.$$
$$CO(x, y, p, t_2) . \supset . Pr(p, y, t_2) = n.$$
$$n > m.$$

The following is an example: a patient has the suspicion that he has skin cancer. He consults his doctor who, after the examination, tells him "you have skin cancer". This statement has a certain degree of probability as related to the state of knowledge of the patient before the communication; but, after consultation with the doctor, the probability of the statement increases considerably. For that reason the doctor is an epistemic authority for the patient in this field.

A word closely related to "epistemic authority" is "competence". One is said to be competent in the field γ if and only if he has a sufficient knowledge in γ. It will appear, however, that by the mere fact that someone is competent in a field, he is not necessarily an authority for all subjects in that field. For, given 6.11, the probability of every proposition communicated by an epistemic authority increases in relation to the state of knowledge of the subject. But this is not the case when the subject is equally or more competent in that field.

6.2 *Justification of epistemic authority*

The acceptance of epistemic authority, i.e., the assumption that the communication of a proposition belonging to a certain field increases its probability, must be justified in some manner. It seems that there are three ways in which this can take place.

(1) *Justification by trust*. In some cases the authority of a person is accepted owing to the trust which the subject has for it. No rational justification is present in such an instance. When a completely unknown man, who is accused of a crime, affirms his innocence and supplies details concerning his actual behavior, he is sometimes trusted, that is, accepted as an epistemic authority in the field of propositions

pertaining to his behavior. Since there is no rational process involved, this sort of justification is completely outside the province of logic.

(2) *Inductive personal justification.* Other cases arise where authority is accepted because several propositions belonging to the same field and communicated by the bearer in the past have been verified as true. The reasoning involved takes the following form: $p_1, p_2 \ldots p_n$, all belonging to γ and communicated by x, are true; therefore, every proposition belonging to γ and communicated by x is probably true. An experience that what a person said about postage stamps, for example, was usually true, establishes his authority in the field of philately.

(3) *Inductive social justification.* In some cases the authority is accepted not because the bearer himself is known to be competent in the field, but because he belongs to a class of men whose competence is recognized. This fact is established by inductive reasoning, similar to the preceding type. The scheme is as follows: $x_1, x_2 \ldots x_n$, all belonging to α, communicated respectively the propositions $p_1, p_2 \ldots p_n$, all belonging to the field γ, and all of which are true; therefore, for every x, if x belongs to α, x is probably an authority in γ; but x belongs to α; therefore x is probably an authority in γ.

An example is medical authority which is attributed to anyone who is a member of the class of physicians. If, on a train or plane, a passenger becomes ill, any doctor – even completely unknown to the other passengers – will be accepted as an epistemic authority just because he is a doctor.

It may be noted that the preceding first premise is itself often based on authority. Thus, even those who have little to do with doctors, will accept their authority because others have told them that propositions communicated by one or another member of the class have been verified as true.

It should also be clear that this sort of justification is usually weak. It is inductive, even based on a series of inductions, each employing a fallible logical rule. Hence the medieval rule "authority is the weakest among arguments".

6.3 *The existence of epistemic authority*

What has been said about the existence of authority in general (§ 4) fully applies to epistemic authority. It might be noted that the concrete examples used in order to illustrate the theorems concerning it were all cases of epistemic authority. Among its existential theorems we shall restate for EA the theorem 4.23:

6.31 $\quad\quad\quad\quad\quad\quad (x)(\exists y, \gamma) EA(x, y, \gamma).$

Everybody is the subject of someone's epistemic authority in some field.
This is a rather euphemistic formulation of the situation. In fact, in the actual state of civilization, everyone is the subject of someone's epistemic authority in very many fields. Specialization of knowledge has developed to the extent that the theorem is obviously true. It may even be said that, as far as our knowledge is concerned, we rely in *most* cases upon epistemic authority: the physician's, the mechanic's, the newspaperman's and so on.

6.4 On rationalism

A doctrine called "rationalism" appears to be a variety of anti-authoritarianism: namely, it is anti-authoritarianism restricted to epistemic authority. Its partisans claim that epistemic authority should not be recognized, which actually means that epistemic authority cannot exist.

On closer inspection this claim seems to be ambiguous. At least five different meanings can be distinguished:

(1) *There is no epistemic authority at all*

$$(x, y, \gamma) \sim EA(x, y, \gamma);$$

this is equivalent to

$$\sim(\exists x, y, \gamma) EA(x, y, \gamma),$$

i.e., to the denial of an analogon of 4.27 and is certainly false.

(2) *There is only one kind of epistemic authority: science.* This means, presumably, that only scientists can be bearers of EA. However, this too may mean several things:

(a) *Only specialists can have EA in a certain science.* This is logically true within the framework of the present theory.

(b) *For every field there is a class of scientists who alone can have authority in it.* This is an existential statement which would have to be empirically justified. It seems that it is not so justified.

(c) *Only scientists may have EA in any field.* Again, and in view of 6.11, this is an empirical statement which must be empirically justified. Once again, however, it appears not to be so. Occasionally, the class of scientists concerned is further restricted as, e.g., to the class of natural scientists or to that of specialists in a certain field.

(3) *There is EA, but only if its acceptance is rationally justified.* No particular method of justification is excluded, as long as it is rational. The difficulty consists in the meaning of "rationally"; whatever the case, justification on trust seems to be excluded.

(4) Finally a still weaker meaning may be distinguished: *epistemic authority is not a valid argument against statements established by other methods.* The reasonableness of the medieval maxim: "auctoritas est debilissimum argumentum" is apparent, given the weakness of the inductive arguments upon which epistemic authority is usually grounded. But this is not always true. Other methods, used in order to establish the probability of a proposition, may sometimes be weaker than those on which the acceptance of authority is based.

6.5 *On epistemic egalitarianism*

Another ideal, which does not coincide with rationalism, may be mentioned, namely, what will be referred to as "epistemic egalitarianism." It can be described as follows: the state in which

$$(x, y, \gamma) \sim EA(x, y, \gamma)$$

is admittedly not present but is an ideal toward which we should direct ourselves. It differs from rationalism in its first meaning (6.4 (I)) is so far as the latter asserts that there *is* no EA, whereas egalitarianism aspires to it. Were that state to be achieved, all men would possess at least one divine property, namely that stated in 4.52: no one would be their EA. Following the situation described in § 6.3 this would seem to be a rather curious sort of utopia.

7. DEONTIC AUTHORITY

7.1 *Definition*

The concept of deontic authority is linked with that of *aim*. In general the situation may be described as follows: the authority of x is accepted by y in the field γ when y desires a certain event e, and the acceptance of the authority is necessary in order to realize e. But the acceptance of the authority is the same as the acceptance of every rule belonging to γ and communicated with assertion by x to y.

We write "$DS(y, e)$" for "y desires e" and "$R(e)$" for "e is realized." We obtain

7.11 $\quad DA(x, y, \gamma) \equiv: (\exists e) : DS(y, e) : R(e) . \supset . (p) . p \in \gamma .$
$CO(x, p, y) \supset AC(y, p)$

x is a deontic authority for y in the field γ if and only if, for all rules belonging to γ and communicated with assertion by x to y, adherence to those rules by y is the necessary condition for an event desired by y. From this, by negating both sides, we obtain

7.12 $\quad {\sim}DA(x, y, \gamma) \equiv: (e) : {\sim}DS(y, e) . v . {\sim}(p) . p \in \gamma .$
$CO(x, p, y) \supset AC(y, p).$

Consequently, if someone rejects deontic authority, he either does not desire the aim in question or believes that obedience to the authority is not a necessary condition for the desired aim, or both.

7.2 Sanction and aim-authority

DA can be divided in two ways. The first division corresponds to the nature of the desired aim. It is based on the following considerations. In every human action a twofold aim can be distinguished: one is the immanent aim or the aim immanent to the action itself (*finis operis*, abbreviated as "*ia*"); the other is transcendent with respect to the action, it is the ulterior aim of the agent (*finis operantis*, abbreviated as "*ta*"). The first is always conceived by the agent as being a necessary condition of the second. Consequently, in all cases we have

$$ta \supset ia.$$

This applies to every action, including those ordered by DA. In such a case two situations may be present. Either the situation (1) where the *ta* of the bearer differs from that of the subject, as happens when the subject accepts the authority because he desires to avoid a sanction (punishment); or (2) where the *ta* of the bearer and the subject are identical. The first kind will be called "sanction-authority" and the second "aim-authority."

Two examples will help to illustrate the distinction. The slave master orders the slave to clean his reception room. The ordered action has an *ia*, namely, the being-clean of the said room. But the slave master and the slave have different *ta*. While the former desires the room to be cleaned because he wants to give a party, for example, the latter is ill-concerned about the party and accepts the authority of the master only in order to avoid punishment. This is a case of sanction-authority. On the contrary, when a flying crew, engaged in a difficult and dangerous flight, accepts the DA of the captain, the *ta* of both the bearer (the captain) and of the subjects (the other members of the crew) is identical: the safe operation of the aircraft. This is a case of aim-authority. We shall denote sanction-authority by "SA" and aim-authority by "AA". In both cases the general structure is the same, namely, that described by 7.11, but in each case the desired event is different according to the kind of authority.

The following theorems seem to hold:

7.21 $(x, y, \gamma) : DA(x, y, \gamma) . \supset . SA(x, y, \gamma) \vee AA(x, y, \gamma):$

every deontic authority is either a sanction-authority or an aim-authority. The "or" is not exclusive since it often happens that both appear together:

7.22 $(\exists x, y, \gamma) . SA(x, y, \gamma) . AA(x, y, \gamma).$

Perhaps this is the case of the taxpayer, who is subject to the sanction-authority of the head of the tax office. Some people, however, pay their taxes not *only* because they wish to avoid fines; they are also motivated by a common aim. Analogous cases would be found in the field of military rules, etc.

7.3 Distributive and non-distributive authority

The second division arises in what may be called "distributive" and "non-distributive authority." In the first instance, the acceptance of every rule belonging to the field by *all* individuals concerned is a necessary condition for attaining the aim. In the case of non-distributive authority this is true of *most*, but not all, subjects.

Suppose a team of workers, each of whose tasks is essential for the success of the common enterprise, as in the aforementioned example of the flying crew. Then the realization of the aim depends upon the strict adherence to the rules by all subjects. However, there are often cases where this is not necessary. Many a war has been won in spite of the fact that some soldiers deserted, i.e., did not adhere to the rules communicated to them. Similarly, many states function and even flourish financially in spite of recurring fiscal frauds. It should be noted that the concept of distributive authority is involved in the definition of the Kantian categorical imperative. This problematic, which belongs to moral philosophy, will not be developed here although it may be pointed out that a correct formulation of that imperative requires an analysis of deontic authority.

8. ON FREEDOM

8.1 Existence of deontic authority and freedom

Problems of the existence of deontic authority are problems concerning the existence of freedom since (political) freedom is nothing other than the non-existence of that sort of authority. However, questions relating to it are usually stated in a way different from those relating to epistemic authority. While for the latter the question of *fact* is most important, the former raise no doubts whether there *is* such an authority. The issue is rather what *should be*, i.e., the question of an ideal state of human relations.

As in all similar fields, logical analysis seems to be needed. Such an analysis will therefore be proposed, followed by a look at some of its ideals.

8.2 Definition of freedom

Basically, freedom is a binary relation between a subject and a field. It can be defined by DA, but as this can be either a sanction-authority or an aim-authority, there are two different kinds of freedom: freedom from every authority and freedom from sanction-authority alone. If someone is free from all deontic authority he is also free from aim-authority. These will therefore be denoted by "FA" for "freedom from all deontic authority" and "FS" for "freedom from sanction-authority". The definitions are:

8.21 $\qquad FA(y, \gamma) \equiv (x) \sim DA(x, y, \gamma):$

y is free in the field γ if and only if no one is a deontic authority (any sort of authority, including aim-authority) for y in γ. The negation of this freedom is defined by:

8.22 $\qquad \sim FA(y, \gamma) \equiv (\exists x) DA(x, y, \gamma):$

y is not free in γ if and only if there is at least one person who is a deontic authority for y in γ.

The second sort of freedom is defined as follows:

8.23 $\qquad FS(y, \gamma) \equiv (x) \sim SA(x, y, \gamma):$

y is sanction-free in γ if and only if no one is a sanction-authority for y in γ. The corresponding negation is defined by:

8.24 $\qquad \sim FS(y, \gamma) \equiv (\exists x) SA(x, y, \gamma)$:

y is not sanction-free in γ if and only if there is at least one person who is a sanction-authority for y in γ.

Both of these notions can be generalized by forming the concepts of absolute freedoms. We shall write "GFA" and "GFS" respectively. Contrary to FA and FS these freedoms are not relations but absolute predicates, such that GFA(y) and GFS(y):

8.25 $\qquad GFA(y) \equiv (x, \gamma) \sim DA(x, y, \gamma)$

8.26 $\qquad GFS(y) \equiv (x, \gamma) \sim SA(x, y, \gamma)$

If these are negated we obtain:

8.27 $\qquad \sim GFA(y) \equiv (\exists x, \gamma) . DA(x, y, \gamma)$

8.28 $\qquad \sim GFS(y) \equiv (\exists x, \gamma) . SA(x, y, \gamma)$

y, in the first meaning of the term, is absolutely free if no person is a deontic authority for him in any field; in the second meaning, he is absolutely free if no one is a sanction-authority in any field.

8.3 On Totalitarianism

With the aid of the preceding definitions, some political ideals can be analysed. One can be called "totalitarianism." It claims that there should be no freedom. However, as there are two meanings of the term "freedom," this may mean either that there should be no freedom at all, or that there should be no freedom from sanction-authority. The first can be formulated as the desire that:

(1) $\qquad (y, \gamma) \sim FA(y, \gamma)$

which, by 8.21, entails

(2) $\qquad (y, \gamma)(\exists x) . x \neq y . DA(x, y, \gamma)$:

for all subjects and fields there is at least one person who is their deontic authority. But in fact it seems that totalitarianism claims a much stronger statement, namely:

(3) $\qquad (\exists x)(y, \gamma) . x \neq y . \supset . DA(x, y, \gamma)$:

there is at least one person who is a deontic authority for everyone else in all fields. Whoever rejects totalitarianism defined in this way must hold that:

(4) $\quad\quad\quad (x)(\exists y, \gamma).x \neq y. \sim DA(x, y, \gamma).$

Usually, however, anti-totalitarians acclaim another ideal:

(5) $\quad\quad\quad (y)(\exists \gamma)(x) \sim DA(x, y, \gamma):$

for every subject there is at least one field in which no one is his deontic authority.

A second variety of totalitarianism is a view, according to which the ideal is:

(1) $\quad\quad\quad (y, \gamma) \sim FS(y, \gamma)$

(2) $\quad\quad\quad (\exists x)(y, \gamma).x \neq y \supset SA(x, y, \gamma)$

there is at least one person who is a sanction-authority for everyone else in all fields – which is by far the stronger statement.

While totalitarianism has usually been understood by its adversaries to claim the second sort of ideal, it is difficult to ascertain exactly what it is that totalitarian leaders really want. In any case, they usually make determined efforts in order that subjects accept their authority willingly, i.e., as an aim-authority.

8.4 On Anarchism

Another view, which will be labelled "anarchism," considers as an ideal the state in which there would be no deontic authority at all:

$$(x, y, \gamma) \sim DA(x, y, \gamma).$$

Whoever rejects anarchism defined in this way must hold its negation as an ideal:

$$(\exists x, y, \gamma) DA(x, y, \gamma).$$

It may be remarked that anarchism and totalitarianism, while mutually exclusive, are not contradictorily opposed: there are 24 intermediary ideals. Without enumerating all, only one will be formulated which seems to be adhered to by many politicians, namely:

$$(y).(\exists x, \gamma) DA(x, y, \gamma).(x)(\exists \gamma) \sim DA(x, y, \gamma):$$

for each person there is a field in which someone is his deontic authority as there is a field in which no one is his deontic authority.

AN ANALYSIS OF AUTHORITY 83

9. ON BELIEF AND DEONTIC AUTHORITY

In this chapter the following problem will be discussed: can a rule prescribing the acceptance of a proposition belong to a field of deontic authority? In other terms, can its acceptance be ordered by such an authority? It may be argued that it can, for the acceptance of a statement is an action which adheres to a rule of behavior, and deontic authority concerns such rules. As a matter of fact, numerous bearers of deontic authority do prescribe such acceptance. The problem is a complex one and its solution requires a distinction of several meanings of "accepts".

9.1 *The meanings of "accepts"*

Insofar as propositions are concerned, "accepts" can have two quite different meanings. "y accepts p" may mean either (1) that y knows (with some probability) that p, or (2) that without knowing anything about the truth-value of "p", y wishes to act on the assumption that p, e.g., in order to verify or refute it.

This can be illustrated by the following example. A pilot flying VFR across a high mountain ridge intends to cross the pass Nr. 1. He finds that it is closed by clouds. However, he knows that 20 miles to the left there is another pass, Nr. 2. He turns to the left. Why? Because he accepts the proposition that Nr. 2 is probably open. But this acceptance may be twofold: either (1) he knows by previous experience and/or by the authority of other pilots that when Nr. 1 is closed there is a probability that Nr. 2 will be open; or (2) he knows nothing about Nr. 2, i.e., he does not know if it is probable that it is open, but wants to try, i.e., to verify it. In the first case there is belief, while in the second it is absent.

On the other hand, a distinction must be made between (1) the acceptance itself and (2) the emotional attitude under which it operates. Quite independently of the fact that a proposition has been accepted either because of its probability or only for pragmatic reasons, the degree of emotional adherence to it may vary. References to "weak beliefs", on one hand, or to statements such as "he believes it passionately", on the other, are common. It may be noted that such typical emotional adherences may be, at least in some cases, the result of a free decision.

9.2 *Theories of belief*

The immediate problem is whether a subject can freely decide to accept a proposition; for, if he can, this decision may be made for him by a deontic authority. In what follows let "y believes 'p' at t" be defined by "y accepts 'p' by a free decision". This is not the current use of the term "believes" in English. However, it will be useful for the purposes of this study.

With the preceding distinctions in mind, it appears that there are three classes of theories according to which y believes 'p,' i.e., decides that:

(1) 'p' is probably true
(2) 'p' has to be assumed for pragmatic reasons
(3) 'p' has to be adhered to firmly.

Theories of class (1) will be called "voluntaristic", while those of classes (2) and (3) "pragmatistic" and "emotionalistic" respectively.

In each class five different theories can be distinguished, according to the probability of p as related to the state of knowledge of y at t, hence: $Pr(p, y, t) = k$. Thus, we may have:

(a) $k = 1$ p is certain
(b) $1 > k > 1/2$ p is more probable than ~p
(c) $k = 1/2$ p is as probable as ~p
(d) $1/2 > k > 0$ p is less probable than ~p
(e) $k = 0$ ~p is certain

Consequently, there are $3 \times 5 = 15$ possible theories of belief.

Of these theories, the voluntaristic can be discarded as false immediately. This is evident from the following. At a time t_1 the probability of 'p' as related to the state of knowledge of y is, let us say, m. Then, at a later moment t_2, y decides something about 'p'. By the fact of that decision nothing has been changed either in p or in the state of knowledge of y. Consequently, the probability of 'p' as related to the state of knowledge of y at t_2 is exactly the same as at t_1. This means that the decision about 'p' is completely irrelevant to it, the decision has no influence at all on the probability of 'p'.

As to the pragmatic theories, even the most radical among them seems plausible, namely, that which asserts that y can accept 'p' for pragmatic reasons even if 'p' is certainly false.

Finally, in regard to the emotional theories, a distinction appeasr necessary. It is difficult, in fact, to imagine someone adhering firmly to a proposition he believes to be false.[6] Consequently, only those theories claiming a degree of probability for their propositions as a condition of firm adherence, may be accepted.

9.3 Belief and deontic authority

A rule can belong to the field of deontic authority if and only if it can be freely accepted by the subject; therefore, the preceding statements concerning the theories of belief entail the following conclusions as to the legitimacy of deontic authority in our domain:

1. *No deontic authority whatsoever – not even divine authority – has in its field a rule prescribing the acceptance of a proposition as true or probably true.* This entails that the ordering of such acceptance by a purely deontic authority is always a misuse of authority in the first of the two meanings distinguished in § 1.3.

The conclusion seems so obvious that one may wonder, how does it happen that bearers of deontic authority (military or religious superiors, for example) impose such rules. The solution to this puzzle lies perhaps in the confusion between epistemic and deontic authority.

2. *A rule prescribing the acceptance of a proposition for purely pragmatic reasons may belong to the field of deontic authority.* Belief cannot be prescribed, but practical considerations may impose the assumption of the rule. In that case, supposing the bearer has DA in the field in general, there is no misuse.

3. *Deontic authority can have in its field rules prescribing the emotional adherence to a proposition, provided that (1) such an adherence is submitted to a free choice, and (2) the proposition under consideration has at least some probability (> 0).*

---

[6] Therefore the saying "credo quia absurdum," attributed to Tertullian (but not found in his works; see however *De Carne Christi* 5, 4) is itself absurd, even if "credo" is interpreted as an emotional adherence.

THEOLOGY AND THE CHURCH'S TEACHING AUTHORITY AFTER THE COUNCIL

KARL RAHNER

On the 24th of July Cardinal Ottaviani as Pro-prefect of the Congregation for the Propagation of the Faith sent a letter to the chairmen of the bishops' conferences. This letter, which was originally intended to be confidential, was concerned with certain tendencies and dangers in modern Catholic theology and in the Church's theological mentality. Evidently the confidential nature of the letter could not be preserved. Very soon larger or smaller reports or excerpts appeared in the press. Consequently it was decided at Rome to publish the letter in the *Acta Apostolicae Sedis*.[1] As a result it is available to everyone and has thus also become an object of public reflection and discussion.

The content of Ottaviani's letter to the bishops is as follows:

The letter begins with the assertion that it is the task of the whole people of God now to really translate into action what has been decided at the Second Vatican Counsil in matters of doctrine or discipline.[2] The letter continues that it is the task of the episcopate to watch over, to lead and further this 'movement of renewal' begun by the Counsil (one may add that all three tasks are to be attended to equally). This must happen in such a way that the genuine unfalsified content and intention of the Vatican documents and decrees is respected in every detail. It is the task of the bishops themselves to protect this doctrine since they are held to have a real commission of authoritative teaching under Peter as their head. However, it is to be regretted that news has come to Rome from various parts of the Church concerning abuses in the interpretation

---

[1] cf. *AAS* 58 (1966), pp. 659–661.

[2] We would commend this statement – issued by such high Church authority and by a man who is entirely above the suspicion of indiscretely craving for novelty – above all to those circles in the Catholic Church in Germany (e.g. certain of the '*Una voce*' groups) who apparently regard it as their privilege to defend ancient truth and hallowed tradition, and who under certain circumstances are not afraid to attack representatives of the Episcopate with most ridiculous suspicions.

of the Council's doctrine and irresponsible opinions, appearing here and there and causing not a little confusion in the minds of many of the faithful. Of course it is imperative to distinguish properly between the deposit of faith and any other opinions; consequently all attempts to understand the doctrines of faith better are to be encouraged. But from the reports of learned theologians and from the study of published theological works the Congregation has become aware of not a few theories which 'to a certain extent' affect dogma and the fundamentals of the faith itself and are no longer keeping within the limits of a legitimate freedom of opinion and hypothesis.

The letter then gives instances to support this observation, emphasising explicitly that it is quoting *examples* of these 'errors', not giving a balanced and exhaustive description of these theological dangers. *Ten* of them are enumerated.

1. Concerning revelation: recourse to scripture with an intentional exclusion of tradition, including the restriction of biblical inspiration and the infallibility of scripture, and the false evaluation of historical texts. 2. Concerning the doctrines of the faith: here and there people are of the opinion that dogmatic formulas of faith are so much involved in the flux of historical development that even their objective import can change. 3. Concerning the teaching office, especially the Pope: it is often so neglected or slightly regarded that it is almost seen as a matter of opinion. 4. Concerning the existence of an objective, absolute, firm and unchangeable truth: certain people practically refuse to acknowledge such a thing and subject truth to a kind of relativism, asserting that truth must necessarily follow the rhythm of the development of consciousness and history. 5. Concerning Christology: certain concepts are used in the re-examination of Christology which are hardly compatible with defined dogma; a 'Christological humanism' is spreading (*serpit*), reducing Christ to the level of an ordinary human being who only gradually became aware of his divine sonship; the virgin birth, miracles and even the resurrection are only held verbally, and in actual fact are made into purely natural matters. 6. Concerning sacramental theology: quite apart from the other sacraments, in the case of the Eucharist certain facts are overlooked or not sufficiently attended to; certain people, pursuing an exaggerated symbolism, proceed as though there were no transubstantiation, but only a kind of 'trans-signification'; the truth of the sacrificial aspect is unjustifiably neglected. 7. Concerning the sacrament of Penance: besides the neglect or denial of the per-

sonal confession of sin, some people conceive this sacrament as a 'reconciliation with the Church' without emphasising sufficiently that it is also a reconciliation with God. 8. Concerning Original Sin: there are those (*nec desunt qui*) who attach little value to the teaching of the Council of Trent or interpret it so that Adam's original sin and the transmission of the guilt of sin itself become obscured. 9. Concerning moral theology: not a few are spreading error concerning the objective nature of morality, denying natural law, advocating a situation ethics and corrupt opinions on the morals of sex and marriage and human responsibility in this field. 10. Concerning ecumenism: however much all the work done in this area is to be praised in its encouragement of love and unity with the separated brethren, the Apostolic See (!) regrets that there are people who wrongly interpret the conciliar Decree on Ecumenism and understand ecumenical work in a way which detracts from the truth of the unity of the faith and the Church in a dangerous indifferentism and irenism.

Finally the letter observes that the errors and dangers which are propounded and incurred in individual instances here and there have been set before the bishops in this short summary so that each bishop can concern himself with overcoming or preventing them in accordance with the duties of his office.

As one can see, there is no mention of particular countries where these errors and dangers can be observed particularly. Although the ten points quoted are said to be examples, their theological compass is so wide (more or less explicitly) that practically the whole of theology can be subsumed under their headings except the question of God and modern atheism. Ostensibly the letter is concerned only with dangers and errors of Catholic Christians[3] and theologians, but one may wonder here and there whether in fact it was not also aimed beyond this sphere at Protestant theology or bore in mind the echo which the latter has had among us, which, though not in a tangible written form, is revealed in many people's attitude of mind and in oral theological discussion. The text scarcely discloses whether the extent and urgency of the errors and dangers are regarded as greater in particular topics or whether they are all roughly equal in this respect.

---

[3] The Protestant Church is itself suffering even more from the issues raised here, as is clearly shown, for instance, in Bishop Hanns Lilje's Pastoral Letter: 'Hirtenbrief über den Kirchentag', *Lutherische Monatshefte* 5 (1966), pp. 462–470 (cf. in the same issue of the journal Bishop H. Meyer, 'Theologie und Gemeinde,' pp. 470 ff.). Naturally, however, we cannot discuss this different situation here.

It is the intention of this essay to set forth a number of theological observations which arise or are at least possible from reading this letter. They can only be discussed very generally here as it is clearly impossible in a short essay to deal with the themes raised by the ten errors and dangers referred to.

I.

First of all let us make one or two observations concerning the spiritual and intellectual climate within which Ottaviani's letter is to be read. It is one of a certain insecurity and perplexity. To admit this is not unworthy of a Christian nor of authority in the Church. There are questions which are of great import and yet for which no immediate answer is forthcoming. A situation can be opaque; it can have many levels; it can be difficult to weigh up the individual tendencies, currents and opinions or to know when a particular thing is perhaps loudly proclaimed in the Church and yet remains peripheral and uncharacteristic of the majority of theologians and Church people. It can be hard to recognize what is a short-lived fashion, due to disappear of its own accord, and what is the beginning of a more serious danger to come; or what is only theology making up for lost time with rather a lot of noise because it was previously dominated by a stagnant theological conservatism, which stubbornly and in fear isolated itself from the real questions. Consequently it remains difficult to say where tendencies appear which really threaten the faith of the Church. The letter does not attempt to draw a veil over this situation of uncertainty. It draws attention to complexes of problems and questions, gives warnings, but does not reach any really doctrinal decisions, not even of a preliminary kind. That is quite within the rights of the Congregation for the Propagation of the Faith. Indeed, it is its duty.

In addition there is this: today it is in the first place never merely a question of repeating the ancient truth, presenting it authoritatively and saying No to deviations from it. We are concerned with presenting this truth in such a way that it really 'speaks to' men and is accepted willingly as being intrinsically true. Whatever the formal doctrinal position may be, it is not sufficient in actual fact to refer back to the formal juridical authority of the Pope and the bishops. Whether we wish it or not, we are subject to the necessity of finding a way between, on the one hand, a 'monolithism'[4] to which everything was clear and

[4] The reader is asked to excuse our using a word from the realm of politics in this context.

where at least anything of any importance could be decided on easily, unambiguously and, above all, quickly and was in fact so decided in a papal declaration of some kind (Encyclical, papal address, declaration from the Holy Office etc.), and on the other hand the tangled chaos in which theologians and laymen feel that in matters of faith they can think and say anything and everything they wish.

The first way is no longer possible as it was pursued previously. It is clear that Vatican II preferred a different method, was more careful and reticent in dogmatic pronouncements, gave more scope to 'dialogue' within the Church, and allowed the different theological currents to be expressed in a less inhibited manner. It has been shown that in many questions an unequivocal and obligatory doctrine can be less easily formulated than was thought to be the case twenty years ago. Complexes of questions, theological terminology and methods have become so diverse in recent decades that it has become much more difficult to say exactly what a theological idea really means when it is 'translated' into another theological language – a task which is necessary, however, in the modern theological pluralism.

The second way, for a Catholic understanding of the faith and the Church, is a false path: there must be a confession of faith in the Church; it is not the case that there are merely equally valid 'interpretations' of the most diverse, disparate or even contradictory kinds in the Church, behind which the common 'meaning' is found only as what is unutterable and inexpressible. There is an authoritative teaching office which is able to express the Church's faith in genuine human conceptuality as true and binding on everyone. It can reject a contrary affirmation and can command assent in saying that such an affirmation is contrary to the truth, however much all the Church's expressions of faith on the one hand point in the direction of the incomprehensibility of God, and on the other hand include the element of congruity within a community of language which could be otherwise.[5] Naturally it cannot be our task in this short essay to provide a foundation for this 'inbetween' situation in a theological theory of knowledge or even to give

---

But it seems briefly and clearly to characterise a particular way in which Church authority (which is not simply identical with the rights and duties of the *magisterium* itself) used to react before John XXIII and the Second Vatican Council. This attitude, which prevailed since Pius IX and above all since the fight against Modernism, may have been justified in its time, but it is nowadays no longer appropriate to the situation and must change, precisely so that the *magisterium* can exercise its function effectively.

[5] cf. K. Rahner/K. Lehmann- *Mysterium Salutis I*, ed. J. Feiner/M. Löhrer (Einsiedeln, 1965), pp. 686–703, esp. 693 ff.; cf. *ibid.*, pp. 727–782 (literature).

practical rules for following this *'via media'*. In this area much remains to be done.

The tendencies and views mentioned by Ottaviani do exist. They exist in the German-speaking world too, although not all in the same degree of clarity. Of course these views do not exist as a complete system. Nor can all the dangers and errors be found to the same extent in German theological literature. It is rather that many of these things are present in the form of a particular mentality, or only come to light in private oral discussion. Naturally these tendencies are clearly expressed in Protestant theology except in the case of specifically Catholic themes like transubstantiation for example. So it would be very remarkable if they were absent from Catholic theology in the German-speaking world (especially today when both theologies influence each other much more than ever before). We have these tendencies too. We shall not illustrate this with individual references, since in the first place it by no means depends on how far the tendencies and attitudes mentioned have found expression in actual theological literature. But we must observe (1) that, as we have said, these tendencies have certainly not been formulated as a 'complete system'; and (2) that there are also questions not mentioned in the letter, although they are just as important (if not more so), which must be attended to. The question of God, of the possibility of experiencing him, the question of atheism and all that is connected with atheism as its foundation – these too belong among the problems which find themselves in a situation of insecurity.

The individual spheres of problems referred to in the letter are also (though not exclusively) concerned almost always with genuine questions and obscurities, with the difficulty of finding a genuine synthesis of the inheritance of faith with what constitutes the modern mentality and with the new questions and insights of the theological and profane sciences. Consequently nothing is effected by giving a simple 'No' to all this and by repeating traditional doctrine of which even the very formulation is monotonous to the ear. This was often stressed by the Council too. But Ottaviani's letter makes rather too little mention of this. In addition the letter's treatment of the issues is unfortunately marked by a vagueness, inevitable to a certain extent, but which is not very helpful. One is obliged to say this in all modesty and openness, even while bearing in mind that this letter was a request to the bishops and did not intend to be a long exposition of theological doctrines.

For instance, when is the *vis inerrantiae et inspirationis* incorrectly 'constricted' (*coarctant*)? For there *is* a legitimate and necessary drawing of boundaries. When is the objective meaning of a dogmatic formula wrongly altered? For there *is* a movement of change in theology which, for instance, purifies the enduring meaning of a dogmatic formula of accompanying misunderstandings which were previously almost inevitable, or which separates it from interpretations which were previously not so clearly distinguishable and now may be freely discussed.[6] When has the doctrine of the Church' steaching authority been undervalued? For there has been progress in theological knowledge (in the last century too) which has caused reformable doctrines of the teaching office to be recognised as being also *de facto* to be reformed.[7] When has there been a false relativism? There exists a development and a history of doctrine, which cannot be interpreted merely as the result of new supplementary items of knowledge but which understands the ancient, 'enduring' truths in a new way. Which new concepts are being tried out in Christology which are incompatible with the Christological definitions? For there is in Catholic theology a process of rethinking of Christology, which is clearly necessary and must work with a modern conceptuality without incurring theological censure. When has the definition of 'transubstantiation' been damaged, when is the concept of '*Agape*' *plus aequo* emphasised at the expense of 'sacrifice'? These are certainly many obscurities in the doctrine of original sin, but when can one speak of 'obscuring' the doctrine if biblical aspects are stressed which are not clearly visible enough in the traditional doctrine? If we are right in rejecting a 'situation ethics' (which?; and what does it imply?), what is the sound core which it does have and which is not sufficiently clear in traditional moral theology? What are the *perniciosae opiniones* in modern sexual morality and how can they be distinguished from the good elements of progress beyond the teachings of Pius XI and XII, which have doubtlessly been accepted or at least prepared for by the Council? When and by what means is a correct ecumenism perverted by a false irenism and indifferentism?

One cannot deny that the tendencies and dangers mentioned in the letter actually exist. Nor can one say that a letter of this sort, or the Church's teaching office in Rome, could do much more than giving this kind of very general warning. But it is precisely this which reveals

---

[6] cf. K. Rahner, 'Zur Geschichtlichkeit der Theologie,' *Integritas*. 'Geistige Wandlung und menschliche Wirklichkeit,' ed. D. Stolte/R. Wisser, *Festschrift für K. Holzamer* (Tübingen, 1966), pp. 75–95.

[7] One only needs to consider the concrete example of evolution (in relation to the concept of Creation, etc.).

the situation: modern theology inevitably deals with a mass of problems and methods of conceptual expression and is so weighed down by the awareness of the ambiguity of all statements that it is not so easy as previously to replace a real or suspected error with another, positive and unequivocal statement in which men of goodwill recognise that not only something correct is said but also something which is equal to their 'concern'.

The situation must be looked at and appreciated soberly; for only then can one ask how the Church and her teaching authority relate in the most correct and effective way within this situation. It is a situation of a pluralism of scholarly theological methods and terminologies, an inconceivable breadth of scope of theological problems, in the face of which no individual theologian can be an adequate specialist at all. For this reason the theologians' theses are no longer simple Yes or No answers to a doctrine which has been traditionally handed on and is fixed and formulated, equally familiar to all, but they are often related to the particular doctrine in a uniquely disparate way. These theses are mostly formulated in a 'dialogue' with philosophies, profane theorems, world-views, which are themselves ranged quite disparately beside one another and are not known and understood in their plurality by any one individual. However much one must always strive to speak with *one* language, to understand each other mutually, these attempts have material limits today. The attempt to produce an absolutely homogeneous theology from the point of view of terminology and the questions it deals with, accessible to all theologians, if it could succeed at all, would end up as the theology of a small sect, unable to address itself to its environment any more. In addition, this situation is characterised and made more difficult by the fact that not a few contemporary Christians maintain in themselves a strange 'unity' of two attitudes: on the one hand the tendency towards 'reinterpreting' doctrine, often with little respect for authoritative Church doctrine, whereby the desire for novelty easily dominates over the preservation of what is permanently valid in ancient doctrine, and on the other hand the desire to stay in the Church and to make room within it for one's own understanding of the faith. If one may put it crudely: before, one simply said No to an affirmation of authoritative Church doctrine and left the Church; now one tries to interpret this doctrine in one's own way and desires it to become commonly held in the Church. By this over-simplified but not insignificant description of the situation we do not mean that authoritative doctrine needs no interpretation but only to be simply repeated, precisely in order that it shall remain and be believed. But the question is, what are the limits of such an interpretation? What are the limits which cannot be exceeded, so that the Church may have the definite courage to say No when they are exceeded, and that the proposer of the interpretation may have the courage and honesty to leave the Church, whose confession of faith he can maintain only verbally and not according to the actual issues? We cannot here answer the question as to how this peculiar 'unity' of two such opposed attitudes is to be explained. In brief one might say perhaps that this 'unity' is symptomatic of the transition from an individualistic to a 'collectivist' age. People (still) wish to think individualistically and yet belong to a community of a similar mind. We cannot deny that such an intention has its justification and is – correctly understood – a task for a meaningful future. The question is only how both can be joined in one in a genuine manner.

II.

In a situation like this, which will surely last for a long time, the former ways and means of doctrinal leadership are evidently insufficient. Today all authoritative representatives of doctrinal world-views (not only the Catholic Church) are faced with the question of how the unity of the obligatory doctrine can coexist side by side with the much quicker development of knowledge in freedom, and how those who make authoritative decisions in these matters are to respond in this situation.

There has been as yet far too little reflection on this matter. The letter also seems to be a symptom of this now inevitable embarrassment, which is, however, without doubt a healthy sign: one is rightly aware that one cannot do simply everything and commit everything to the 'free discussion' of 'autonomous scholarship', and at the same time one cannot see precisely how and what one is to decide clearly, in order that the decision is both correct as far as the particular issue is concerned and also effective.

It is here that the bishops themselves have a task, so that they need no longer simply wait for authoritative decisions or 'doctrinal political' measures from Rome, as was mostly the case before, content to be relieved of this difficult office of teacher in the modern Church by the Congregation for the Propagation of the Faith. Here we see a strange convergence between the theoretical teaching of Vatican II concerning the bishops' teaching authority, which they possess *iure divino* and on which they must themselves lay hold, and the concrete situation which calls for such a teaching authority. The bishops cannot pass on this task of theirs either to the authorities in Rome or to the theologians.[8] What the dogmatic constitution of the Church of Vatican II said about the office of a bishop is not to remain mere pious print. Furthermore it would be highly dangerous if Rome's effectual authority – the effectiveness of which is not unlimited – were over-taxed. The bishops can address themselves to a particular, regionally diverse situation with better prospects of actual effectiveness than Rome. For while Pius XII was in office Rome did not always procede sufficiently carefully and sympathetically, with the result that (if we are seeing things as they unfortunately are) it doubtless lost a certain amount of effective authority even among those who were not in principle opposed to this doctrinal authority. Therefore that authority of the bishops which is humanly speaking more effective in particular concrete circumstances, should not be by-passed. It can be more effective – in the human sphere above all – because it can react more appropriately to a concrete situation, confronting and appreciating not only opinions but also those who hold them. It is, or could be, therefore practically speaking more capable of dialogue. Ultimately too it is more effective since, being the penultimate authority, it can 'risk' more (and should have the courage to do so).

In not a few cases the clergy must understand more clearly than before that by no means everything which is discussed in theological science is also suitable for the pulpit. The pulpit is not the proper place for dubious 'demythologisings'. This distinction does not imply in any way that the preacher may say things in the pulpit which he could not defend before the honest and truth-seeking conscience of the scholarly Church theologian. The distinction is based on insight into the sermon's purpose: the salvation of man in the concrete, of the man who is listening and who can be hurt even by what is, in the abstract, a correct statement, if it is said wrongly. Indeed, the letter itself says that the bishops themselves are to do something about this and not merely make reports, and to this extent the letter is 'post-conciliar' in the best sense.

One ought to try as far as possible to foresee doctrinal and practical

---

[8] It is interesting to observe the parallel situation that Bishop Lilje too has to defend himself against the accusation that he is not exercising his episcopal teaching authority (cf. *supra*, p. 85, note 3).

developments, to lay hold on them in good time and direct them into right paths, separating what is inevitable and correct from what is extreme, eccentric and mistaken. Many of these tendencies which are just becoming apparent to us will very soon become more pronounced and more threatening. We must take that into account quite soberly. The questions which are also raised in the letter will be asked more loudly and more publicly; e.g. the question of 'error' in scripture; the relationship, in theory and practice, of the man who is both Catholic and theologian to non-definitive decisions of the Church; the manner of knowing God; the nature of original sin; the virginity of the Mother of God; the meaning of God becoming man etc.; also the more practical questions of life and piety will become more urgent, e.g. the concrete forms of the Eucharist (Benediction, 'visits', processions, Exposition) ; of the confession of devotion; of sexual morality; of mixed marriages; the ethics of education (confessional questions concerned with schools); the celibacy of the secular clergy etc. We can imagine that these and many other similar questions will be asked more insistently and clearly everywhere in the foreseeable future. Something ought to be done in this respect in good time. If false views have already become entrenched and are proclaimed loud and clear in the Church's public consciousness, it is already almost too late. But much is still possible now, at the beginning of the development. It should therefore be actually taken in hand. Nothing is gained by a fearful, deadly silence.

In this matter it is inadmissible to think that everything is clear and that only muddle-heads have new problems with the old questions, which have been answered clearly long ago. For instance, there still seem to be canonists (and bishops too?) who proceed as though a Catholic is morally not permitted – by virtue of divine law – to contract a particular marriage if the children cannot be guaranteed a Catholic upbringing. That is incorrect.[9] Or it is thought to be completely left to the Church's discretion – not only according to canon law, but also morally – under what conditions a mixed marriage may be permitted. That is not right. The question of the 'infallibility' of scripture has not been answered and solved by the Council alone in such a way as to do real justice, in a positive manner, to the legitimate difficulties and problematical situations of the exegetes (and nowadays of the laity too). The question of Christ's knowledge concerning himself is one for

---

[9] Details in the *Handbuch der Pastoraltheologie* II/2 (Freiburg, 1966), pp. 99–103; also the thorough study by J. G. Gerhartz, 'Die Mischehe, das Konzil und die Mischehen-instruktion,' *Theologie und Philosophie* 41 (1966), pp. 276–400.

which the exegete demands a better answer of the dogmatician than before, in order to deal with his problems. Nowadays, in spite of '*Humani generis*', one may surely be permitted to assume that a theory of polygenism does not contradict the doctrine of original sin as defined at the Council of Trent. But this ought to be substantiated in greater detail and it ought to be shown that a polygenism of this kind does not require such a reinterpretation of the doctrine of original sin which would dissolve the dogma effectively into a weak rationalism. The doctrine of original sin must be re-thought no less in other points too, even if one is obliged to respect completely the teaching of Trent on this issue. The open questions in practical sexual morality are well known. Text-book theology has often arrived at an answer too easily. What degree of moral maturity is needed to constitute an indissoluble marriage is a dark question, and its answer has very practical consequences which the canonists have by no means been considering clearly enough or long enough. There are plenty more examples like this.

In many cases Rome itself will only be able to give a 'skeleton answer' (like the Council). Such an answer is important. But it is often not sufficient to protect the orthodox doctrine in a way which does not demand an unjustified *sacrificium intellectus* or permit the propounding of actual heresy or theological error under cover of an apparent verbal respect for authoritative doctrine. A certain formal and juridical mental attitude which one finds in Rome (and which is understandable and even unavoidable) cannot deal on its own with this situation, in the first place because, as the final authority of the whole Church, it cannot easily speak the theological and human language which is appropriate and understood in a particular cultural setting.

The bishops have a task here; but they must recognise that a solution has yet to be found and cannot be presumed at the outset. Furthermore the solution must not be present simply anywhere, but must be communicated to the general awareness of the clergy, in order to protect the latter from either reactionary or heterodox 'solutions'.

In the face of this situation of open questioning, the clergy in the first instance, but also the laity, must be made far more clearly aware than before that an attempt at a solution made by individual theologians in the Church is not automatically acceptable in respect of dogma – seen from a practical point of view – if it is presented by a personally respectable theologian and has received the episcopal *Imprimatur*.

Today it is absolutely impossible to discuss such problems *in camera caritatis*, excluding all public participation and exposing only the matured solutions to the public gaze. Here too it is no longer possible to conduct 'privy council politics', although that does not mean that any theological nonsense ought necessarily to be allowed to pass the episcopal censure. It is quite in order and necessary for the episcopal censuring authorities to be magnanimous and tolerant in the case of scholarly publications (and conversely stricter than usual with pseudo-pious products which are only apparently 'popular'). In the case of scholarly theological literature the episcopal censor should be limited to a 'coarse filter', simply because it is scarcely possible today to do otherwise without obstructing necessary theological discussion. The latter is indispensable today even in important theological questions, not only in questions which have been regarded as 'open' (and of no consequence) from time immemorial. If that is the case, however, it must be clear to the clergy (especially the young clergy) and laity that in actual fact an *Imprimatur* gives no definite guarantee of the objective reliability of the view expressed. Consequently it may be a theologian's right and duty to question the orthodoxy of another theologian's theory, even if the latter were published by episcopal permission. Of course, a challenge of this sort is stated at the particular theologian's own risk and carries only as much weight as the reasons he gives. But it can be permitted or even invited. In so far as this does not happen enough, the wrong opinion grows up that everything which appears beneath an *Imprimatur* is orthodox and may not be doubted. Because this false view prevails the episcopal censors are obliged to become more anxious and rigorous. As a result the theologian's function with respect to the ecclesiality of a new attempt at a solution of a theological question is excluded, to the disadvantage both of the issue itself and of episcopal authority, which consequently has to be over-strained. It is a false politeness and collegiality when theologians are too concerned to take pains to be 'indulgent' with one another. The indisputable decline in theological criticism is to be deplored in this respect, and it is an extremely dangerous situation.

One must not imagine that in relatively weighty theological questions there can or ought to be no continuing differences of opinion which even the Church's teaching office cannot resolve (at least after a lengthy period of time). The Council has declared the reverse to be fundamentally the case, and has given concrete examples of it. One could quote cases – even in post-conciliar Germany – where this freedom in disputed questions has not been sufficiently respected by Church authorities.

However, it must not be thought that today one can either leave each question alone or that it can be cleared up in a purely scholarly dialogue with the agreement of all theological parties, without the teaching office having to step in authoritatively. The bearers of doctrinal authority (each according to his fundamental and respectively different authority and according to the importance of the matter in hand) must have the courage to say No under certain circumstances, even if they have not been able to 'convince' each and every person beforehand by exhortation, theological discussion of the issue itself, etc. After all, the Church *has* a common confession of faith which must be protected; the Church is more than a theological debating society; furthermore it is not possible to distinguish what is purely 'fundamental' from what is 'secondary', guarding the former and unconditionally surrendering the latter. The sense of the Decree on Ecumenism No. II is that there *are* things which, although not fundamental or only peripherally so, all the same constitute indisputable dogma in the Catholic Church. On the other hand even what is fundamental is under certain circumstances threatened nowadays by erroneous interpretations, even if they are able to maintain a certain verbal reverence for Church definitions. What is 'indispensable' and what is not is decided in the final analysis by the theology of the *magisterium*, not by the theology of the theologians. The latter have, however, an irreplaceable function in the Church, such that today the bishops have less right than ever before to make decisions simply on the basis of what they learned at one time in some fashion or other, but must keep on continually informing themselves anew. We have already mentioned that in having the courage to take such a decision they must not only make the one which is correct according to the matter in hand, but must also proceed in a humanly understanding and 'winning' way. In this latter respect the bishops have moral duties as well; and it cannot be so readily assumed as people would sometimes have us think that these duties are objectively fulfilled.

Since the bishops are obliged, in the modern complexity of theological problems, to have recourse to advice from theologians, and since the Spirit's aid to the Church is not exclusively available to the bishops and to no others, the bishops will have the right, and under certain circumstances the obligation, to let a theological view go uncensured when it is supported by a considerable body (and this need not be a numerical majority) of theologians who have demonstrated their competence by their teaching and life in general. Certainly this rule presupposes that the bishops have the practical possibility of knowing when a view is present (and what it concerns) which is subscribed to by a considerable section of theologians who think it correct or open to discussion. On the other hand not every opinion of an individual is immune to episcopal objection simply because the particular individual is respectable from the human and scholarly points of view. Naturally every theologian maintains that his view (as being correct or open to discussion) is the result of theological 'science' or some other science, and everyone is only too tempted to regard himself as the mere spokesman of this particular objective 'science'. But that on its own need by no means keep back the bishop in his teaching office from saying an unequivocal 'No' in certain circumstances.

More of these rules could be set up and refined 'casuistically', but ultimately no rule can relieve the bishop of his 'decision' in the specific sense of the word. Ultimately he must decide according to his knowledge and conscience how much courage he needs to use his authority and what measure of caution must be prescribed for using it in the concrete instance. If, objectively speaking, he prescribes wrongly, he can act wrongly in either direction. But he must have the courage to take this risk all the same. He has no absolute security against such a contingency. It is not pleasant, where matters of truth and the intellectual integrity of individuals is concerned, to have to come to a decision under certain circumstances knowing that the decision cannot be regarded as 'irreformable'. But human life and the Church's life of faith are not thinkable without these vulnerable and yet valid decisions. Even theological scholars for the most part do not get beyond such provisional decisions – which are all the same valid here and now – even where they are pronounced under the strange conviction of being merely mouthpieces of 'objective science'. So the right to make decisions of this sort is all the more to be granted to the official authority. For the faith and the Church are not made in the theologian's retort, but are carried by apostolic proclamation in the message which is entrusted primarily to Church authority, to the bishops. The vulnerability of reformable decisions of this kind does not excuse the office-bearer from exercising the duty of his office. But the 'censured' theologian cannot at the outset fundamentally refuse to accept the decision of the bishop's teaching authority and guardianship simply because it is not *a priori* above the possibility of error, not 'irreformable'.

III.

What measures can be taken practically to do justice to these – self-evident – observations and rules? To this question we shall give a merely partial answer in question form.

How can collaboration between bishops and theologians become concretely closer? Why does not the episcopate provide the highly somnolent 'dogmaticians' study groups with tasks, by giving particular advice and suggesting important themes for conferences, etc.? (The same applies to the similar 'society of exegetes'). In the late Middle Ages and in the sixteenth century there were more institutions than today through which theologians expressed themselves as unities and bore collective responsibility. Today it is surely even more necessary. Surely the practice of theologians acting as consultants for the commissions of the bishops' conference ought to be more clearly institutionalised, so that it actually functions correctly and one knows who is responsible for giving advice?

Ought not the episcopal book censorship to be reformed? And why in our case is the provision of canon law not observed whereby the censor has to be responsible by name for his decision? Ought he not to do this when a book is rejected too? Are the censors always competent? Are they both courageous and cautious? Is it certain that the preliminary censure has still more advantages than disadvantages today, or does it not lead to false evaluation, i.e., an over-valuation of those books which have only just passed the censor? Would not other forms of episcopal reaction to theological work and views be more effective and appropriate today?

Is it not necessary today for the episcopal teaching office (in addition to agreeing to the appointment of professors and the filling of similar posts, sermons, the pastoral letters which for the most part seem rather antiquated, and the episcopal book censorship) to be exercised in other ways, best of all perhaps as the official statement of a bishops' conference? E.g., by the bishops' conference issuing teaching letters and publishing its recommendations etc.? Theoretically the bishops' conference has for a long time had an institution for implementing the work of critical and productive contact with theology today and current cultural life as it is theologically relevant. One sees little sign of it and is tempted to doubt whether this institution, as it appears to exist, is even capable of informing the episcopate adequately on all these questions. Is it sufficiently provided with the necessary personnel and technical equipment for such a task?

Could not the 'priests' council' which is to be formed in the individual dioceses be in addition an instrument for keeping the bishop informed about doctrinal tendencies and unrest among the clergy, and for instructing the clergy correctly on such questions? Are the possibilities provided by deanery conferences, theological conferences for priests, conferences for Catholic academies (why not also for members of the clergy themselves?) sufficiently exploited for the purposes we have mentioned? Could not the bishops, without interfering with the free play of theological scholarship by excessive direction, influence the specialist theological journals to apply themselves more to modern questions of theology than to merely learned historical research (the importance of which we do not contest)?

Are the bishops really sufficiently aware of theology's urgent need of their encouragement at an academic level? Are all the bishops definitely willing enough to choose carefully and make available people who will eventually take up theological lectureships? Can this still be left to the individual bishop? May it still happen that a bishop refuses to free theologians for further study on account of a shortage of priests, in the hope that another bishop will do so in any case? Is it not possible to believe that the future of Christianity and the Church will be better served by a highly educated and lively clergy, able to deal with the mentality of our time, than by a quickly trained clergy prematurely expended in the routine work of the care of souls?

Is it not the case that educated people in the Church are very defectively taught by the mass media as regards theological questions? We do not mean to recommend that a more anxious watch be kept over religious broadcasting etc.; that would be quite out of place; but it is possible to have the impression that the bishops do not make available people of high enough qualifications for such a task. Is one not struck by the fact that in a broadcast religious discussion the lay contribution is often better and more relevant than what is presented by the Church in a narrower sense?

The solution of the problems referred to by Ottaviani will depend in the future largely on the training of young theologians. Is the new programme of studies which was committed to the bishops' conferences by the Council being pursued energetically enough? In practice is it not in danger of withering away or being wrecked by the specialist egoism of the individual professors? Are people aware that under certain circumstances professors, who are only exalting their own subject, do not make good advisers in the reform of studies, especially if, as is sometimes the case, they do not understand very much about modern pastoral care, the mental outlook of young people and the level of intelligence of the people who are nowadays coming to theology? So far what has been made known as a result of deliberations about the reform of theological studies in Germany seems merely like a tedious bargaining over lecture timetables. Do people seriously think that this is enough? If the subjects studied are left as they are, unless the ultimate aim, i.e., the training of future pastors, emerges more clearly than heretofore as the principle of form and organization of the studies, unless the actual level of intelligence of the young theologians is more realistically taken into account, unless the theologian's academic instruction is brought into a closer relationship with the existentially religious forming of his personality, the reform of studies will collapse.

Is it not possible to come to a clearer understanding as regards those questions touched on in Ottaviani's letter? How does one transform a mere defence against erroneous or dangerous views and tendencies into a theology of 'offensive'? Could not the bishops encourage such a theology (and not just tolerate it benevolently) where traces of it are to be found?

Without diminishing the Church's basic duty to conserve and defend the whole inheritance of faith, has not the Church's teaching authority the right (and perhaps the duty), trusting in the inner power of Christian truth, to organise centres of concentration instead of fighting battles on all points and frittering away its not inexhaustible resources of strength, gaining a victory nowhere? It ought not be thought that man has always to be doing 'here and now' all the things which he *could* do. For instance one *can* fight false views regarding the theory and practice of Indulgences; but the fight against atheism, conducted properly, is certainly a more pressing problem.

Would it not be possible to pursue quite generally a more offensive theological 'cultural politics' (in the best possible sense), with bishops and theologians more clearly forming a community than is the case at present, where theologians constitute merely the critical element and the bishops represent merely the conservative element in the Church? – a strategy in which the theologians themselves take a clearer part in the offensive of defending the Church's doctrine, and the bishops' role is more clearly that of critically examining this same doctrine. Collaboration between bishops and theologians proved its worth at the

Council. Will it be continued, or will everything back in the home situation, after the passing of the Council, remain as it was before the Council?

Everything that has been said is to be understood as a few observations upon Cardinal Ottaviani's letter. It would be truer to say that the letter has provided the stimulus rather than the subject-matter of these remarks. For it is plain that our observations have not entered deeply into the individual theological problems enumerated in the letter. They are thus concerned with a preliminary area of discussion. It may be that some readers have the impression that these notes hover between 'reaction' and 'progress' in theology.[10] But perhaps the author may hope that such an impression is fundamentally a false one after all. Not every compromise is dishonourable. Insight and action are always aiming for a centre which cannot be reached directly. For many, the extremist cuts a better figure than the one who continues patiently to seek this centre anew. But there is need today of that patience which seeks the centre.

---

[10] On the serious and difficult nature of the questions posed by the Council cf. the author's essay 'The Second Vatican Council's Challenge to Theology,' in *Theological Investigations*, Vol. IX. New York: Herder and Herder, 1972, pp. 3 ff.

AUTHORITY

Frederick J. Adelmann

Let us begin this discussion with a descriptive definition which refers to the general notion and yet does not specify exactly what authority is. In this sense authority is that phenomenon necessary in a community to get any kind of constant, unified action from the persons involved in order to attain the goals of the society.[1]

Immediately we must distinguish between authority and one of its usual concomitant factors, namely, coercion. Coercion means unwilling force – either physical compulsion, moral threats, psychological brainwashing or social conformism. Consequently, coercion can be internal or external; violent or suggestive; but in any case it does not leave the person affected free to make his own compliance.

On the other hand, authority *in se* is something quite different inasmuch as it is a power of will that causes a response of will in another. This response is a form of obedience, not blind but reasonable.

To clarify further the meaning of authority, let us consider a few generally accepted instances of this notion.

1. Persons who believe in God, believe that He possesses authority – as creator, provider and ultimate judge. He issues certain commandments at the basis of religions. Thus, Abraham was willing to sacrifice his son Isaac because God demanded it. This is one of the best examples known of what is meant by faith in God and the implications of His authority.

2. A father makes certain demands on his children. He does not merely suggest or wish compliance but in certain cases demands it. The father-image is a true authority-image. Several years ago a college student related to me that his father told him that he did not want him to use marijuana – because it was harmful to his health, inevitably led to the

---

[1] Chester Barnard defines authority as "The character of communication (order) in a formal organization by virtue of which it is accepted by a ... member of the organization as governing the action he contributes: that is, as governing or determining what he does or is not to do so far as the organization is concerned." Chester Barnard. *The Functions of the Executive.* Cambridge, Mass.: Harvard University Press, 1938, p. 163.

use of hard drugs, was against the law – and finally because I don't want you to do it. The son replied: 'I can put bullet holes in every one of your arguments except the last, and as a matter of fact – because you don't want me to smoke pot – I won't." This is an example of authority.

3. Civil society functions on the basis of authority regardless of what form it takes. There have been democracies, monarchies, bureaucracies and unfortunately dictatorships and police states. But all have claimed to possess authority over their subjects. The opposite of authority in this sense, at least, is anarchy. Anarchy has never existed for a very long time in any society for it brings about the dissolution of any enduring or extensive social community. Today we hear much about structural anarchy or participatory democracy but even in these cases there is admittedly authority, yet it is only different in the sense that it is supposed to work from the bottom up and is more vague than other known forms.

Many forms of government in the concrete depend on coercion rather than on the moral power of pure authority. Indeed, today, we hear little about the spiritual or moral power of authority. Rather technological society covers up its coercive power by public relations, advertising, the media and fear.

4. The Church, or I might say, any religious institution is in some sense authoritative in its commandments, ritual and administration. Often, however, authority in its true sense becomes bogged down in administration so that its true spiritual sense is lost.[2]

5. There is a lesser kind of authority in existence that is really a derivative of the civil society and yet is truly authoritative as for example, in our schools and colleges, in the police and military. Yet these types are less universal in their applications than the more general kinds so far mentioned. Nonetheless, officials in these groups claim the right to make certain demands on others.

6. Finally, there is a more refined or confined type of authority found in associations, industry and in academic circles. Thus, club members must follow their rules, workers must take orders from a foreman, and scholars usually accept the accepted data of scientists or humanists who have acquired a reputation in their field. In fact, in daily life

---

[2] "Authority commands, always involves the power of the leader to bring the group along and is a natural part of any organization, including the Church." James Drane. *Authority and Institution*. Milwaukee: Bruce Publishing Company, 1969, pp. 15-16.

everyone who wears a uniform is regarded as possessing some limited authority.

Let us now reflect on this data and try to discover some common and distinctive qualities pervading the exercise of authority. For a moment let us prescind from the authority of God because it is unique and would involve a discussion of religious faith. But in the other cases, we find that authority always occurs between persons in some kind of community. This implies a certain communication between the persons, which, in turn, involves modes of symbolization usually through language but sometimes through gestures or other symbols such as a flag or a uniform. Furthermore, the exercise of authority occurs not just within a group of persons but within a group that has a common purpose that requires unified activity by the members. Hence, aside from the divine authority, the common goals of all other groups are limited in their influence over a person's conscious life.

Finally, an authoritative verbal communication has a certain necessity about it. This means that its final decisions are not open to further debate or to be argued about or rejected. Discussions of pros and cons are usually necessary, healthy and natural, but once the authoritative command has been issued it ought in a moral sense to be obeyed. The discussion or debate prior to the decision is not the authoritative dictum. Of course, there are various kinds of authoritative decisions, some serious, others less important. But the decision of one in authority is not a mere wish but a will-act; it is not a mere suggestion but a command. It is obligatory, i.e., binding but on a free subject who must freely respond by a self-initiated reaction in the sense that the act is under his control. Sometimes one's wishes are merely indicated but if the one in authority is acting authoritatively he expects compliance.

What is being emphasized here is one of the most important and characteristic aspects of an authoritative act. In other words, the direct discourse implies the content of the action – the immediately rational part that could perhaps be argued about. But what makes the communication authoritative is not the content of the direct discourse but the mode of the indirect discourse. For example, one who speaks authoritatively does not say: "I would like you to do such and such"; or "I suggest" or "I wish" but he implies "I will it." Indirect discourse introduces us to the intentionality of the speaker, over and above the direct statement issued. Thus to say, I know that he is a thief, leads one to believe that the speaker has other evidence than the merely stated fact. The core of authority resides in the indirect intention and not in the direct discourse. And the indirect intention is that he wills. Hence to argue about the reasons for or against the direct discourse is quite aside from the essence of authority. And the intention, then, is always a willed intention on the part of the one giving a command.

Now, of course, what one wills should not be irrational or without previous deliberation about the wisdom of the direct discourse. Since, moreover, there is a bi-polar relation of persons involved in the exercise of authority, the response expected necessarily in the other person or persons ought to be a personal, free, rational response just as the authoritative command presented is supposed to be so qualified.

Undoubtedly, it is difficult for one to realize that he can give a necessary response and believe that it is free. But in the question of the human will a distinction must be made between the spontaneous will-acts that emanate from our person in a free way and the other form of will-acts that have to do with free choices of means based on a deliberative process.[3] Man can be free in both of these acts. Aristotle brings this distinction out clearly when he discusses the case of the mariner in a storm who is forced to cast his cargo overboard to save his life and the ship. He certainly would not have made such a choice under ordinary circumstances, yet he now freely does it, in fact while he freely does it, he would prefer not to be doing it. But it is certainly a human, free act. In other words, in the light of a wider context, the rationality or irrationality of the particular action becomes at the moment irrelevant, due to a kind of necessity deriving from the contextual source. Thus, St. Thomas, Spinoza and Hegel can all speak about one aspect of freedom in terms of the recognition of necessity. Indeed, we all freely act this way in following a proper diet or a doctor's prescription.

Albeit, someone will rightfully object how can I be free and rational unless I see the rationale in the order commanded. The answer is that the rationale does not have to come from the direct discourse but may emanate solely from the context of the indirect discourse. In other words, the willed intention of the one commanding has its own rational basis. Although authority is proximately a will-act in both parties, it is not separated from reason because willing does not occur in a vacuum. Willing and reasoning are co-related. The intellect forms the

---

[3] Cf. Jean-Paul Sartre. *Of Human Freedom*. Edited by Wade Baskin. New York: Philosophical Library, 1966, p. 41. "In any case let us remember that the will is determined within the compass of motives and ends already posited by the for-it-possibilities. If this were not so, how could we understand deliberation, which is an evaluation of means in relation to already existing ends?"

content, the will executes, moves. The will moves and guides the reasoning process; it moves the lips and the gestures. The one commanding is both willing and reasoning, and the one obeying is both willing and reasoning. Authority is not simply a reasoning process but a willing that wills others to will too.

Usually, in the exercise of authority, the reasons of the one giving the command can be accepted as correct and valid; or an opportunity is given for debate and discussion until some agreement is reached. But, not always so, as for example, when an air-line pilot gives a command to his passengers. They obey without debate and whether they see the reasons or not because he has a title to command them in the situation. We need not rehearse a litany of examples but just as no one has a right to yell "fire" in a crowded theatre so too, a president can give an order without every citizen discussing his right to do so in our modern complicated society. This point then, is to realize that anyone acting authoritatively must have a clear title to the exercise of that authority.

Probing deeper, we ask what is that title and where does it come from? The title is a power of will coming from outside a person, yet bestowing by its impact a new power within him to exert his will power outside of and beyond himself on other persons and expecting a will reaction of compliance with his decision. The Greek philosophers had a neat way of expressing this difference. A person has a power of self-control called *autexousios* which is distinctive of human persons. It is power of will over the self in many of its activities. But authority is called *exousios* by these same writers in the sense of an ability to express their being outside of themselves. And this seems to refer to a kind of existential power of will over others.[4]

However, knowing what this power or title is in itself, leads us to ask about its source. The answer varies according to the type of community and sphere of influence involved. For example, God has a clear title to his power by his very omnipotence. But other titles come either from nature itself or from agreement among the participants or from a recognized technical knowledge. Actually, this is somewhat oversimplified but I wish to avoid particular details involving the abuse of authority.

Yet the three sources mentioned are generally an adequate bracket

---

[4] See my article, "The Theory of Will in Saint John Damascene," in *The Quest of the Absolute* (Boston College Studies in Philosophy, Vol. I). The Hague: Martinus Nijhoff, 1966, pp. 22-46.

for discussing the origins of titles to authority. For example, a father has authority from nature itself. Human offspring cannot, like fish or animals, be let free to work out their mundane salvation as soon as they are born. In fact, fish are freed from parental control before they are born. But human children by nature must be clothed, fed, reared and educated over a long period of time and, hence, as members of the familial society they come under the parents' title to authority from nature itself. And because the title comes from nature, reasoning plays only a gradual role in the recipients who nonetheless as potential adults must be treated with human respect.

Civil society, considered in the abstract, is a necessity of nature and so ultimately is rooted in the plan of the Creator. Inasmuch as authority is a necessary element of any perduring society, the authority involved in civil society has its ultimate title radicated in God. But in the concrete, any particular form of government existing on the contemporary scene is the result of historical conditions and subject to evolutionary changes. These forms should depend on the will of the members in the continuation of the state as legitimate. In other words, despite the form a state possesses at the present time, if it is denying basic human rights, it becomes illegitimate. But we cannot keep going back into history to find out whether a certain form of government arose originally in a legitimate way. This is unrealistic. Each form of government must be adjudicated as it presently exists. If it possesses *de facto* power, then one must ask – does it exercise this power according to the norms of justice. If so, it has a proper title to exercise authority because it is operating for service. Many contemporary writers, as for example Hans Kueng, believe that authority is only held for service. This is true but superficial. It does not analyze the true meaning of what authority is all about and how it actually operates. In a democracy, this power resides explicitly in the will of the people, and is transferred to its delegates by agreement. Of course, this should always be the case in regard to any civil society, but in a democracy a system for change is legally built into the system; in others change can only occur through a *coup*.

Subsidiary types of authority must also have a clear title to the authority they use in their particular sphere. Thus a dean of a college is limited in the use of authority by the officers of the institution, the trustees approved by the state, and the limitations of authority within the state itself in educational matters. The police and the military have a similar title from the state for a limited use of authority. Clubs and associations which do not rest on natural law, have a limited authority based on the will of members. People are free to enter and leave such associations at will. In the practical order people are not free to enter and leave a civil society at will. It is simply well-nigh impossible to live on this planet today and not belong to some state; hence today at least the state has become a natural, i.e., necessary state of affairs. Whether this is good or bad, it is a fact.

At this juncture, we must emphasize again that authority should never be irrational either on the part of the one exercising authority or on the part of the one expected to comply. As a consequence, in the practical orders, boards of appeal should be set up in all institutional structures, so that wherever possible an independent board could consider the reasons for the authoritative command.

This does not mean that the rationality of authority is lodged principally in the dictate because, in human affairs, we all know how difficult it is to get agreement from everyone on what is to be done. The best that we can do is to safeguard justice. Authority, then, is permanently lodged in the title to the power to influence others. The rationality of the power is, therefore, found in the context and title more than in the actual command or direct discourse. Hence, authority is as much a matter of willing as it is a matter of reasoning.

The dictates of one exerting authority, consequently, are not simple statements, but indirect "oughts" or "musts" and they demand a response of obedience in a person who is as much a will-responder as he is an intellectual assenter.

In this connection I would like to discuss Professor Kenneth Megill's position in his recent book, entitled *The New Democratic Theory*.[5] Megill is one example of a thinker who explicitly denies authority yet implicitly admits it. He refers to the need of organization, discipline and leaders. Admittedly, he has not worked out the solutions to these problems but from what we have seen, they necessarily will imply authority.

It should be noted, too, throughout the quotes that follow from his work the disrepute that democracy as usually understood has come under in recent days. Yet majority rule is probably the best method that we can use, hoping that the majority will give a just response to a question affecting the minority who very often *post factum* is seen to have been right after all. Nonetheless, votes can't be taken on every question; hence, authority is necessary within the wider context of

---

[5] Kenneth Megill, *The New Democratic Theory*. New York: The Free Press, 1970.

the goal. At any rate, here are the interesting excerpts from Professor Megill's book:

"In fact, as an abstract principle, majority rule does not seem to be essential for democracy. Rather what is essential is that the crucial decisions which are made in a social situation are controlled by the members who actually live and work in that organization. The principle of majority rule can have nothing at all to do with democracy and can even serve as a cover for a decision-making process which is undemocratic." (p. 89).

The reader should notice the semantics involved here. Usually in the West, democracy means government "by the people" in the sense of free elections and majority rule. Democracy as used in the Communist countries such as in the German Democratic Republic is understood in the way that Professor Megill uses the term, namely, a government "for the people." Of course, Megill would like to see a kind of grass roots democracy like the current experiment in the Yugoslav Worker's Councils. But, even here, the question arises – how are decisions to be arrived at finally? Thus, one never seems able to avoid the implicit authority necessary in practice, no matter how decentralized we try to establish the forms of governing. Thus the following quotations bring out clearly Megill's quest.

"Not destruction of bureaucracy but its control, is the crucial problem." (p. 108).

"The policy of confrontation with the authoritarian system which has been pursued by the radicals, particulary in the West, has demonstrated that the survival of an authoritarian system ultimately rests on the ability of those in authority to use the police to preserve the existing power relations ... in all bureaucratic organizations authority rests on the ability to apply coercion." (p. 100).

Professor Megill seems to think that all authority rests on coercion. He has no conception of the notion of authority that is basically moral power, to be used only within definite limits and that realizes that its subjects possess the dignity of human persons. And yet he maintains: "Democracy means that the worker has the power to control the decisions which affect him." (p. 101).

One asks in this connection how does the worker control decisions? What kind of power is involved here? Is it coercive or a moral power? And do all the workers arrive at their final decisions by majority vote? And if not, how are these final decisions settled?

"The movement now, at the beginning of its revolutionary phase, is faced with the problem of a proper organization. How can a revolutionary movement exist in an advanced industrialized country? What kind of discipline is necessary for members of the movement? What is the proper relationship of the members of the movement to the leaders? All of these questions are being seriously discussed in the movement as it develops. Organization becomes the crucial theoretical question once it is understood that the current order is producing its own contradictions and there is a concrete possibility for a new order." (pp. 162–3).

In the above quotation the reader can discover that the author has no concrete blueprint for the future. Nonetheless, he indicates the need for organization, discipline and leaders but does not offer any principles for deciding or defining these roles in the new structures. Is it enough to leave the solution "to the theory and practice of the movement as it develops"?

Professor Robert Paul Wolff in his stimulating and profound study entitled *In Defense of Anarchism* agrees with so much of my own analysis that I am going to quote him at length:[6]

"To claim authority is to claim the right to be obeyed." (p. 5).

"Thus authority resides in persons; they possess it – if indeed they do at all – by virtue of who they are and not by virtue of what they command." (p. 6).

"Obedience is not a matter of doing what someone tells you to do. It is a matter of doing what he tells you to do because he tells you to do it. Legitimate, or *de jure*, authority thus concerns the grounds and sources of moral obligation." (p. 9.)

Professor Wolff has some doubts about whether or not anyone possesses authority, but, if anyone does, then he agrees with much of the substance of this paper. For example, authority claims obedience not because of what is commanded but because of the title of the one commanding.

But in the following quotations his divergence from my position is made clear:

"Even after he has subjected himself to the will of another, an individual remains responsible for what he does." (p. 14).

"From the example of the doctor, it is obvious that there are at least some situations in which it is reasonable to give up one's autonomy.

---

[6] Robert Paul Wolff. *In Defense of Anarchism*. New York: Harper and Row Publishers (Harper Torchbooks), 1970.

Indeed, we may wonder whether, in a complex world of technical expertise, it is ever reasonable not to do so." (p. 15).

"For the autonomous man, there is no such thing, strictly speaking, as a command. If someone in my environment is issuing what are intended as commands, and if he or others expect those commands to be obeyed, that fact will be taken account of in my deliberations. I may decide that I ought to do what that person is commanding me to do, and it may even be that his issuing the command is the factor in the situation which makes it desirable for me to do so." (p. 15).

"The primary obligation of man is autonomy, the refusal to be ruled." (p. 18).

"More precisely this individual will have a moral obligation to obey the commands of the mediation or arbitration council, whatever it decides, because the principles which guide it issue from his own will." (p. 25).

"But insofar as a promise of that sort is the sole ground of my duty to obey, I can no longer be said to be autonomous. I have ceased to be the author of the laws to which I submit and have become the willing subject of another person." (p. 29).

"If the individual retains his autonomy by reserving to himself in each instance the final decision whether to cooperate, he thereby denies the authority of the state; if, on the other hand, he submits to the state and accepts its claim to authority, then so far as any of the above arguments indicate, he loses his autonomy." p. 40).

"A promise to abide by the will of the majority creates an obligation, but it does so precisely by giving up one's autonomy. It is perfectly possible to forfeit autonomy, as we have already seen. Whether it is wise or good, or right to do so is, of course, open to question, but that one can do so is obvious." (p. 41).

"... But the citizens have created a legitimate state at the price of their own autonomy." (p. 42).

"However if sense can be made of the notion of moral force, we are still without a reason why the minority has an obligation to obey the majority." (p. 44).

Of course, it is necessary to point out clearly why Professor Wolff comes to different conclusions than I do on the final validity of authority in practice. His reason for denying this validity rests on his fundamental unwillingness to relinquish any personal autonomy. I respond in the following way:

1. A distinction should be made initially between relinquishing ANY

and ALL autonomy. Even a superficial reading of my paper discloses that at no time would I agree to a relinquishing of ALL autonomy.
2. Probing deeper, however, do we relinquish our autonomy according to my thesis? I think not. And my reasons are that autonomy resides principally in the will, and our willful obedience must still be free and rational in any case. If we widen our context beyond the direct discourse and submit to a proper title for the common good, this to me can result in a perfectly free and rational act that is automonous. In fact Professor Wolff seems to imply just this in his own statements where he widens the context beyond the command as the reason for obeying. However, it is to be especially noted that he analyzes authority in terms principally of the will and a subsequent act of obedience.

As a matter of fact, the root of Wolff's unwillingness to agree with my conclusion lies in his denial of any real moral power. This implies a denial of any reality beyond the empirical; a denial of metaphysics. Yet in his discussion Professor Wolff himself implicitly admits such moral and metaphysical realities or else there is no substance left to his own thesis.

Engels gives us a different version of the impossibility of preserving so-called autonomy. However, Engels neglects the moral power much more than Wolff does, not distinguishing authority from coercion. Still he presents some good theory behind the valid notions of authority by introducing the semantics behind many anti-authoritarian arguments. Further, he brings out the important fact that all human authority should be limited. The fear of many is that authority as it has been practised is absolute – a fear that enters the picture because of the denial or neglect of the proper limitations necessary in a metaphysical analysis of authority as a moral power.

Here are the pertinent quotes from Engels' short work "On Authority":[7]

"They demand that the first act of the social revolution shall be the abolition of authority. Have these gentlemen ever seen a revolution? A revolution is certainly the most authoritative thing there is; it is the act whereby one part of the population imposes its will upon the other part by means of rifles, bayonets, and cannon - authoritarian means, if such there be at all; and if the victorious party does not want to have fought in vain, it must maintain this rule by means of the terror which its arms inspire in the reactionaries." (p. 661).

[7] Frederich Engels. "On Authority" in *The Marx-Engels Reader*. Edited by Robert C. Tucker. New York: W. W. Norton and Company, Inc., 1972, pp. 662-5.

"Authority in the sense in which the word is used here, means: the imposition of the will of another upon ours; on the other hand authority presupposes subordination." (p. 662).

"... Everywhere combined action, the complication of processes dependent on one another, displaces independent action by individuals. But whoever mentions combined action speaks of organization; now, is it possible to have organization without authority?" (p. 662).

"Thereafter particular questions arise in each room and at every moment concerning the mode of production, distribution of materials, etc., which must be settled at once on pain of seeing all production immediately stopped; whether they are settled by a decision of a delegate placed at the head of each branch of labour or, if possible, by a majority vote, the will of the single individual will always have to subordinate itself, which means that questions are settled in an authoritative way." (p. 663).

"When I submitted arguments like these to the most rabid anti-authorians the only answer they were able to give me was the following: Yes, that is true, but here it is not a case of authority which we confer on our delegates, but of a commission entrusted! These gentlemen think that when they have changed the names of things they have changed the things themselves. This is how these profound thinkers mock at the whole world." (p. 664).

"... Hence it is absurd to speak of the principle of authority as being absolutely evil, and of the principle of autonomy as being absolutely good. Authority and autonomy are relative things whose spheres vary with the various phases of the development of society. If the autonomists confined themselves to saying that the social organization of the future would restrict authority solely to the limits within which conditions of production render it inevitable, we could understand each other; but they are blind to all facts that make the thing necessary and they passionately fight the word." (p. 664).

Engels, too, locates the essence of authority in the will to command and the reciprocal will of obeying. He notes that any organization requires authority. A close reading of Engels reveals the same semantic weakness of Megill's position that we encountered above.

Let us sum up the salient points of this analysis:

1. Authority as moral, spiritual power is necessary if any group is to perdure for any length of time in the work of attaining certain goals. Of course, several persons can get agreement in a small group or commune for some brief period of time on the working out of their goals.

But inevitable disputes will arise that have to be decided by vote or chance or some kind of authority agreed on.

2. Authority occurs between a dialectic of persons and consequently there must be an agreement about the intrinsic value and dignity of human persons. A person is an incarnate spirit and this implies that a person is self-conscious, rational, free, emotive and living in flesh and blood. It also means that a person can only be adequately defined as needing and working with others and, hence, community is a necessary structure of human existence. Each pole in the dialectic possesses the same human dignity. It follows, then, that the lawgiver, the authoritative person, must act rationally to the best of his ability, and be ever cognizant of the nature and dignity of the persons at the other pole.

3. An authoritative command is principally an act of the will; and its dialectical response is also principally an act of the will – although reason is a concomitant factor in both poles. Yet what specifies authority is the willing and not the reasoning. This will element is denoted by an implicit indirect discourse, namely, "I will that such and such be the case."

4. Such a will-act in the authoritative command must be due to a proper title that is possessed by the authority and known by the correspondent.

5. Some origins of this "power of will" or "title" are nature itself, agreement of the persons involved or special knowledge.

6. The presence of the title must be recognized generally but not always by each individual person at the time compliance is demanded. For example, children or citizens who cannot understand the complexities or have not had an opportunity to properly appraise the situation may only vaguely recognize the title.

7. The title and consequently the exercise of this power is always limited except in the case of the divine power.

8. Since subjects of whom compliance is required, are persons, it follows that they must have reasons for giving this compliance. If we agree with the rationale of the command, we only have extrinsic authority, i.e. the person agrees with the dictum and only receives corroboration from the title of authority. Yet, the compliance ought to be given even when the rationale of the dictate is not recognized, on the proviso that the other conditions of proper title are fulfilled, Thus, the context of command and title furnishes a reason itself so that the subsequent will response is not irrational. In this way the response is a free, spontaneous act of a human person rooted not in a

free choice about means but rather in a free commitment to the end or goal of the society itself.

9. In the final analysis, the subject who is expected to accept an authoritative command is a person who must make up his own moral mind. Authority does not obliterate the responsibility of conscience. Conscience, of course, must be formed, but it remains the final arbiter in every personal decision and to dirempt it, is to destroy the person. No authority can contravene a person's conscience in the moral sphere. But the challenge must be in reference to the title, e.g., is it valid, and for this situation, and in this sphere? Thus, if the command contravenes a higher authority it is invalid. If the command is patently stupid, then there is no true authority, for authority should never be irrational. In the practical sphere, authority usually demands the right to use sanctions, but this is another aspect of authority not essential to this discussion.

Furthermore, each person in the forming of his conscience must possess a hierarchy of values, according to which the limits of various institutional structures also limit the proper exercise of authority. We can conclude by stating that authority requires wisdom on the part of all persons involved and even humility in both parties. But in our day to speak about the virtue of humility turns off most hearers. But if that situation continues, authority will perdure but as mere coercion.

10. The reason for the modern rejection of authority is because persons today believe that it is contrary to personal dignity to ever agree without seeing the reasons. But they falsely limit the reasons to the dictum itself. They do not widen the context to include the phenomenology of the intentions manifest in the indirect discourse. Secondly, infected with an over intellectualization, they think that all problems can be solved by setting down the reasons. They forget the shortcomings of human flesh and blood; they try to settle all problems by logic and computers; they forget the emotions, the intuitions, the traditions and the unknown factors in life itself.

Kierkegaard rejected the Hegelian system because its great rational system could not solve many real human problems. The existentialists of our time have placed the real dignity of man not in reasoning but in willing, and modern youth disgusted with the false progress of a technological way of life has turned to the mystical and even the magical sources of approaches to the problems of the day. At least the way has been opened for a new consideration of ' authority" and its requisite virtues of humility and obedience.